A Concise Ch
Kings and Que
Egypt

GW01451672

NEW KINGDOM PERIOD

18th Dynasty

Including the Princes and Princesses,

Royal Titles, Family Trees and Time Lines

Kemet Scribe Guides

ISBN 13: 978-1511464499   ISBN 10: 1511464496

http://arkpublishing.co.uk/

Bernard Paul Badham

1

King List

17th Dynasty - Second Intermediate Period

Senakhtenra Tao I 1558 BC

Seqenenra Tao II 1558-1555 BC

Kamose 1555-1550 BC

18th Dynasty - New Kingdom Period

1. Ahmose I Nebphetyra 1550-1525 BC

2. Amenhotep I Djserkara 1541-1520 BC

3. Thutmose I Aakheperkara 1520-1492 BC

4. Thutmose II 1492-1479 BC

5. Hatshepsut Maatkara 1479-1458 BC

6. Thutmose III 1479-1425 BC

7. Amenhotep II Aakheperura 1425-1400 BC

8. Thutmose IV 1400-1390 BC

9. Amenhotep III Nebmaatra 1390-1352 BC

10. Amenhotep IV/Akhenaten Neferkheperura-waenra 1352-1334 BC

11. Smenkhkara Ankhkheperura 1334-1333 BC

12. Neferneferuaten 1334-1332 BC

13. Tutankhamun/Tutankhaten Nebkheperura 1333-1324 BC

14 Ay Kheperkheperura 1324-1320 BC

15. Horemheb Djeserkheperura-setep-enra 1320-1392 BC

CONTENTS

The Second Intermediate Period

DYNASTY 17: ROYAL FAMILIES

5

18th DYNASTY

ROYAL FAMILIES

Ahmose I

Page 43

Ahmose-Nefertari + Ahmose-Satkamose + Ahmose-Henuttamehu

Princess Ahmose-Merytamun, Princess Ahmose-Satamun, Prince Siamun, Prince Ahmose-ankh, **Amenhotep I**, Prince Ramose, possibly Mutnefret

Amenhotep I

Page 57

Ahmose Merytamun + Satkamose + Senseneb?

Amenemhat (died young), **Thutmose I**?

Thutmose I

Page 65

Queen Ahmose (mother of Hatshepsut) + Mutnefret

Thutmose II, **Hatshepsut**, Amenmose, Wadjmose, Nererubity

Smenkhkara, Meritaten, Meketaten, Ankhesenamun,
Neferneferuaten Tasherit, Neferneferura, Setepenra, **Tutankhaten**
(Tutankhamun), Ankhesenpaaaten-ta-sherit

Smenkhkara

Page 183

+ Meritaten

Neferneferuaten (Female)

Page 187

+ Nefertiti? Meritaten?

Tutankhaten - Tutankhamun

P191

+ Ankhesenpaaten (Amarna)-Ankhesenamun (Thebes)

Two stillborn daughters

The Tomb of Tutankhamun

The Art & Hieroglyphic Inscriptions

Page 201

Ay

It-Netjer Kheperkheperura

Page 211

Ankhesenamun + Great Royal Wife Tey

Horemheb

Page 215

Amenia + Mutnedjmet

APPENDIX

Page 219

Royal Titles

Foreword

The beginnings of the glorious Eighteenth Dynasty are best understood by examining the pharaohs and events at the end of the Intermediate Period, namely the Seventeenth Dynasty. It was during this time that an important ruling family emerged in the south determined to unite Egypt by expelling the foreign Hyksos rulers of the North.

The Second Intermediate Period

The 17th Dynasty

1580 to 1550 BC

The Fifteenth, Sixteenth and Seventeenth Dynasties of ancient Egypt are often combined under the group title, Second Intermediate Period. The Seventeenth Dynasty dates approximately from 1580 to 1550 BC and covers a period of time when Egypt was split into a set of small Hyksos-ruled kingdoms. The last two kings of the southern Theban dynasty opposed the Hyksos rule over Egypt and initiated a war that would rid Egypt of the Hyksos kings and begin a period of unified rule, the New Kingdom. Kamose the second son of Seqenenra Tao II was the brother of Ahmose I, the first king of the Eighteenth Dynasty.

▶

Royal Family Tree: Rulers at the End of the 17t Dynasty

Ruling Pharaohs are underlined

Senakhetenra Ahmose Tao I + Tetisheri

Seqenenra Tao II Ah-hotep I, Ahmose Inhapi, Sat-djhuty, <u>Kamose</u>

Seqenenra Tao II + Queen Ah-hotep I + Ahmose Inhapi + Sitdjhuty

Kamose, <u>Ahmose I</u>, Ahmose-Nefertari, Henutemipet, Merytamun, Nebetta, Sipair, Tumerisy, Binpu, Ahmose, Henuttamehu

<u>Kamose</u> + Ah-hotep II

Sat Ka-mose

17th **DYNASTY**

18th **DYNASTY**

<u>Ahmose I</u> + Ahmose-Nefertari + Ahmose-Satamun + Ahmose-Henuttamehu

Royal Families

Senakhtenra Ahmose Tao I

S-NAKHET-RA MOSE-IAH

1558 BC

Reign: 1 yr

s-nxt-n-ra di anx

made-strong-Ra given life

S-nakhet-en-ra di ankh

'Strength of Ra, given Life

ms-s-iaH di anx mi Ra

born-moon (god Iah) given life like Ra

Mos-iah di ankh mi Ra

'Born of the Moon (god Iah), given Life like Ra'

Reign: 1 yr?

Predecessor: Sekhemra-Heruhirmaat Intef

Successor: Seqenenra Tao II

Consort: Tetisheri

Children: Seqenenra Tao II, Ah-hotep, Ahmose Inhapi, Sat-Djhuty, Kamose

Father: possibly Neb-kheper-ra-Intef

Died: 1558 BC?

Reign: Senakhtenra Ahmose Tao I was the seventh king of the Seventeenth dynasty of Egypt during the Second Intermediate Period. Senakhtenra reigned for a short period over the Theban region in Upper Egypt at a time when the Hyksos 15th dynasty ruled Lower Egypt. Senakhtenra died c.1560 or 1558 BC at the latest. He is generally believed to have been a member of the family of Ahmose and as such identified with the otherwise unidentified spouse of Queen Tetisheri, Ahmose's grandmother. He was succeeded by his son, Seqenenra Tao II. King Senakhtenra would also be the husband of Tetisheri who is called the 'Great King's Wife' and 'the Mother of my Mother' in a stela at Abydos by pharaoh Ahmose I. Senakhtenra was, therefore, the grandfather of Ahmose I.

Queen Tetisheri

TETI-SHERI

𓏏𓏤𓂋𓅓𓀁 𓅐 𓇳 𓍹𓏏𓏏𓂓𓀁𓇓𓆓𓏛𓆙𓍺

nsw Hmt wrt, nsw mwt (tti-Sri) anx ti DtA

king wife great, king mother (the young-little one) Life she Forever

Nesw Hemet Weret, Nesw Mut (Teti-Sheri) ankh ti djeta

'King's Great Wife, King's Mother,

'The Young One, may she Live Forever'

Spouse: Senakhtenra Ahmose Tao I

Children: Seqenenra Tao II, Queen Ahhotep I, Kamose?

Father: Tjenna

Mother: Neferu

Burial: a mummy found in Tomb DB320 in Deir el Bahri may be hers, but her tomb is unknown, possibly KV41.

15

Stela of Ahmose honouring his grandmother Tetisheri. Found in the ruins of Tetisheri's pyramid in the complex of Ahmose's pyramid at Abydos

Reign: Tetisheri was the daughter of Tjenna and Neferu. The names of Tetisheri's parents are known from mummy bandages found in TT320. She was selected by Senakhtenra, despite her non-royal birth, to be not only his wife but his Great Royal Wife. Tetisheri was the mother of Seqenenra Tao II, Queen Ahhotep I and possibly Kamose. In the stela she is depicted wearing the Mother Goddess headdress of the vulture goddess Mut.

The pharaoh Ahmose I, her grandson, erected a stela at Abydos to announce the construction of a pyramid and a 'house' for Tetisheri. Ahmose refers to the Queen as 'the Mother of my Mother,' and 'the Mother of my Father, Great King's Wife and King's Mother, Tetisheri.'

Tetisheri is often credited as the 'mother of the New Kingdom,' because of her powerful influence on her son Seqenenra Tao II and her grandsons, Kamose and Ahmose I who fought to expel the Hyksos from Egypt and lead the country into a new age of wealth and prosperity. She is also thought to have been the mother of Queen Ahhotep, the wife of Seqenenra Tao II.

Tetisheri was not of royal blood, but her husband went against tradition and made her his 'Great Wife.' In addition to the many titles and privileges given to her by her husband, she became the first queen to wear the vulture headdress of Nekhebet. This crown became an icon which soon became closely linked to the power of the 'Great Wife' as a complement to the power of the Pharaoh.

When her son Seqenenra Tao II rebelled against the Hyksos rulers of Avaris, she spearheaded the recruitment of troops. When her son was killed in action, she supported both Kamose and Ahmose as they continued to fight. She was apparently a valued advisor and confidant for all three kings.

She lived to the grand old age of seventy. During her lifetime, there were numerous decrees proclaiming her services to the Egyptian people. On her death, Ahmose I granted her a great estate and pyramid and mortuary temple with priests and servants to conduct rituals in her honour.

SEQENENRA TA-AA

1558-1555 BC

Reign: 3 yrs

nsw bit, nb tAwy (s-qn-n-ra)

king South King North lord Two-Lands (made-brave-Ra)

Nsw Bit Neb Tawy (S-qen-en-Ra)

'King of the South and the North, Lord of the Two Lands,

Made Brave of Ra'

sA-ra (tA-aA)

son Ra (DHwty-great)

Sa Ra (Ta-aa)

'Son of Ra, Djhuty is Great'

Hr [xa-m-wAst]

Horus [appear-in-Thebes]

Hr [Kha-em-Waset)

'Horus [Appearing in Thebes]'

17ᵃ Dynasty	New Kingdom 18ᵃ Dynasty				
1560 BC	1550 BC	1540 BC	1530 BC	1520 BC	1510 BC
I Tao II Kamose		Ahmose I		Amenhotep I	

Reign: 1558-1555 BC

Predecessor: Senakhtenra Ahmose

Successor: Kamose

Father: Senakhtenra

Mother: Queen Tetisheri

Consort: his sister Queen Ah-hotep I, Ahmose Inhapi, Satdjhuty

Children: Kamose, Ahmose I, Ahmose-Nefertari, Henutemipet, Merytamun, Nebetta, Sapair, Tumerisy, Binpu, Ahmose, Henuttamehu.

Died: in battle or executed

Burial: Mummy found at Deir el Bahri cache

Monuments: Palace and fortifications at Deir el Ballas

Reign: Seqenenra Tao II, called 'The Brave,' ruled over the last kingdoms of the Theban region of Egypt in the Seventeenth Dynasty during the Second Intermediate Period. He probably was the son and successor to Senakhtenra Ahmose and Queen Tetisheri. The dates of his reign are uncertain, but he may have rose to power in the decade ending in 1560 BC or in 1558 BC. With his queen, Ahhotep I, Seqenenra Tao II fathered two pharaohs, Kamose, his immediate successor, who was the last pharaoh of the seventeenth dynasty and Ahmose I, who, following a co-regency with his mother, was the first pharaoh of the eighteenth. Seqenenra Tao II is credited with starting the opening moves in the war of liberation against the Hyksos, which was ended by his son Ahmose I.

Ahhotep I, his wife and sister, was another powerful queen. An ambiguous sentence on a stela devoted to her indicates that she may even have rallied troops:

'She is the one who has accomplished the rites and taken care of Egypt... She has looked after her soldiers, she has guarded her, she has brought back her fugitives and collected together her deserters, she has pacified Upper Egypt and expelled her rebels.'

Tradition states that Seqenenra Tao II had contact with the Hyksos northern ruler, Apepi (Apophis). The tale states that the Hyksos king Apepi sent a messenger to Seqenenra II in Thebes to demand that the Theban hippopotamus pool be done away with, for the noise of these beasts was such, that he was unable sleep in far-away Avaris. Seqenenra II seems to have led military skirmishes against the Hyksos and judging from the vicious head wound on his mummy in the Cairo Museum, he may have died during one of them.

Seqenenra II's mummy was discovered in the Deir el-Bahri cache, revealed in 1881. His mummy was unwrapped by Gaston Maspero who records:

'...it is not known whether he fell upon the field of battle or was the victim of some plot; the appearance of his mummy proves that he died a violent death when about forty years of age. Two or three men, whether assassins or soldiers, must have surrounded and despatched him before help was available.'

The war with the Hyksos did not end upon his death. Instead, his wife-sister Ahhotep I rallied the troops and pushed northward against the Hyksos until their son, Kamose came of age. It was in fact his second son, Ahmose I who finally drove the Hyksos from Egypt and established the 18th Dynasty New Kingdom Period.

The relatively short length of the reign of Seqenenra Tao II did not allow for the construction of many monumental structures, but it is known that he had built a new palace made of mud brick at Deir el-Ballas. On an adjacent hillside overlooking the river, the foundations of a building were found that almost certainly was a military observation post.

Queen Ah-hotep I

HOTEP-IAH

1560-1530 BC

30 yrs

Htp-iaH

satisfied-moon

Hotep-Iah

'Iah (the Moon god) is satisfied'

Father: ?

Mother: Queen Tetisheri

Spouse: husband and brother Pharaoh Seqenenra Tao II

Children: Pharaoh Ahmose I, Pharaoh Kamose, Queen Ahmose Nefertari

Burial: reburied in TT320 in Deir el Bahari

Life: Ah-hotep was the daughter of Queen Tetisheri and Senakhtenra Ahmose Tao I, and was probably the sister, as well as the wife, of Pharaoh Seqenenra Tao II. Ahhotep I had a long and influential life. Her titles include 'Great Royal Wife' and the 'Associate of the White Crown bearer.' The title 'King's Mother' was found on the Deir el Bahari coffin.

She is also thought to have been the mother of the princes Ahmose Sapair and Binpu and the princesses Ahmose-Henutemipet, Ahmose-Nebetta, Ahmose-Merytamun and Ahmose-Tumerisy. When her husband was killed fighting the Hyksos, Ah-hotep rallied the troops and maintained the pressure on the invaders until her son Kamose was old enough to lead the army. A stele in Karnak temple records her service to the nation, stating:

'She is the one who has accomplished the rites and taken care of Egypt... She has looked after her soldiers, she has guarded her, she has brought back her fugitives and collected together her deserters, she has pacified Upper Egypt and expelled her rebels.'

When her second son Ahmose I succeeded in expelling the Hyksos, he led his army to Nubia to regain lost territories. While he was gone, a group of Hyksos sympathisers tried to steal the throne. Ah-hotep foiled this attempt, and was awarded the 'golden flies of valour' by her son. He also gave her a cache of beautiful jewellery and ornamental weaponry which was found in a tomb at Dra Abu el-Naga near the Valley of the Kings. Her original tomb has not been discovered.

The award of the Golden Flies was a military distinction. Golden Flies were awarded to those soldiers who, like flies, attacked the enemy repeatedly.

Queen Ahhotep received splendid ceremonial artefacts after the country was liberated from the Hyksos because of her bravery and support for her late husband and her two sons. The ceremonial artefacts (three golden fly pendants, a battle axe, and two models of ceremonial bark) found in her tomb were part of the funerary and ritual objects used to symbolize and guarantee the eternal victory of the order (Maat, Truth, Order and Justice) over the chaos (the enemies or evil forces).

The ceremonial axe presented to Ah-hotep by her son Pharaoh Ahmose I bears his cartouche name and titles:

'The Good God, Neb-Phety-Ra, Son of Ra Mose-Iah (Ahmose)'

On the axe blade he is depicted slaying one of is Asiatic enemies. Under this is inscribed **mTw mry** 'Montju Beloved' i.e. beloved of the god Montju.   Montju was the falcon headed god of War.

Ah-hotep I's outer coffin was eventually reburied in TT320 in Deir el Bahari. The coffin shows the queen with a tripartite wig. The body is covered in a Rishi-style (feathers) and is similar to the outer coffins of Ahmose-Nefertari and Ahmose-Merytamun.

Ah-hotep I's original tomb is not known.

Queen Ahmose Inhapy

IAH-MOSE-IN-HAPY

~𓅓𓇌𓏥𓈖𓈗

iaH-ms-ini-apy

moon-born-bring-Nile

Iah-mose-in-Hapy

'Born of the Moon, Bringer of the Nile'

Spouse: Pharaoh Seqenenra Tao II

Father: Pharaoh Senakhtenra Ahmose Tao I

Siblings: brother and husband Pharaoh Seqenenra Tao II, and sisters: the queens Ahhotep and Satdjhuti

Children: a daughter named Ahmose-Henuttamehu

Burial: tomb in Thebes, mummy reburied in DB320 near Deir el Bahri in the Theban Necropolis.

Life: Ahmose Inhapy was probably a daughter of Pharaoh Senakhtenra Ahmose Tao I and was sister to Pharaoh Seqenenra Tao II, and the queens Ahhotep and Satdjhuti. She probably married Seqenenra Tao II, but it is possible she dates to the later time of Ahmose I, or even Amenhotep I. She had a daughter named Ahmose-Henuttamehu. Ahmose Inhapy was mentioned in a copy of the Book of the Dead owned by her daughter Ahmose-Henuttamehu, and in the tomb of Amenemhat (TT53). Her titles were: 'King's Wife and King's Daughter.

Queen Sat-Djhwty

SAT-DJHWTY

sAt-DHwty

daughter-Djhuty (Thoth, the ibis headed god)

Sat-Djhuty

'Daughter of Djhuty'

Spouse: half-brother Seqenenra Tao II

Children: Princess Ahmose

Father: Senakhtenra Tao I

Mother: Queen Tetisheri

Life: Sat-Djhuty was a queen and princess of the late 17th Dynasty Period. She was a daughter of Pharaoh Senakhtenra Ahmose and Queen Tetisheri and wife to her brother Seqenenra Tao II. She was also the mother of Princess Ahmose. Sat-Djhuty was a sister to the queens Ahhotep and Ahmose Inhapy. She was married to her half-brother Seqenenra Tao II and bore him a daughter, Ahmose. Sat-Djhuty's mummy was discovered around 1820, along with its coffin, golden mask, a heart scarab and linens donated by her niece Queen Ahmose Nefertari. The linen is inscribed with the text:

'Given in the favour of the god's wife, king's wife and king's mother Ahmose Nefertari may she live, so Sat-Djhuty.'

The fact that Satdjhuty should have received such an honour shows she was a lady of the highest rank in courtly circles.

Princess Henutemipet

Father: Pharaoh Seqenenra Tao II

Mother: Queen Ahhotep I

Burial: Deir el Bahri DB320

Life: Ahmose-Henutemipet was a princess of the late seventeenth dynasty of Egypt. She was a daughter of Pharaoh Seqenenra Tao II and probably Queen Ahhotep I. She was the sister of Ahmose I and she bore the titles 'King's Daughter and King's Sister.'

Death and Burial: Her mummy was found in the tomb DN320. Henutemipet died as an old woman; she had grey hair and worn teeth.

Princess Ahmose-Merytamun

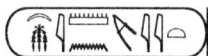

ms-iaH imn-mr-yt

born-moon beloved-Amun

Mose-Iah Meryt-Amun

'Born of the Moon, Beloved of Amun'

Father: Pharaoh Seqenenra Tao II

Life: Princess Ahmose-Merytamun was a daughter of Pharaoh Seqenenra Tao II. Her titles included: 'the Royal Daughter, the royal sister Merytamun.'

Death and Burial: Her mummy was found in the Deir el Bahri cache (DB320). The mummy shows the remains of an old woman who was short in stature.

Princess Ahmose-Nebetta

ms-iaH nbt-tA

born-moon lady-land

Mose-Iah Nebet-ta

'Born of the Moon, Lady of the Land'

Father: Seqenenra Tao II

Mother: Queen Ahhotep I

Siblings: Pharaoh Ahmose I

Life: Princess Ahmose-Nebetta was probably a daughter of Seqenenra Tao II and Queen Ahhotep I. She was a sister of Ahmose I. Her titles include: 'King's Daughter and King's Sister.'

Death and Burial: unknown

Princess Ahmose-Tumerisy

ms-iaH-tw-(mr?)si

born-moon-one-beleved?-she

Mose-Iah Tu(mer?)sy

'Born of the Moon, She is the Beloved One'

Life: Ahmose-Tumerisy was a princess of the seventeenth dynasty of Egypt, probably a daughter of Seqenenra Tao II and a sister of Ahmose I. Her titles were: 'King's Daughter and King's Sister.'

Death and Burial: Her name is known from her coffin, which is now in the Hermitage Museum. Her mummy was found in the pit MMA 1019 in Sheikh Abd el-Gurna.

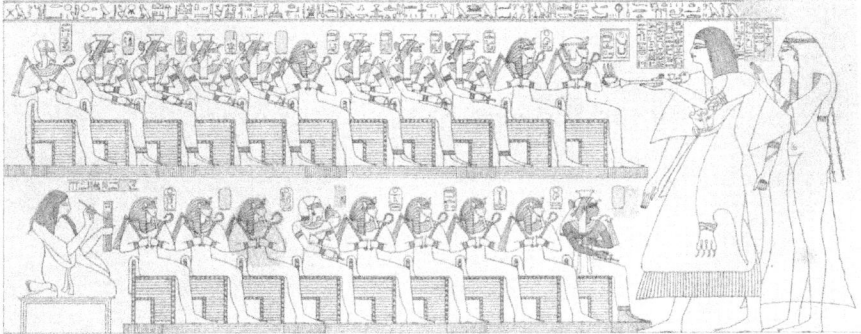

Ahmose Tumerisy in a scene from the tomb of Inherkau (20th Dynasty).

Top row, right to left: Amenhotep I, Ahmose I, Ahhotep I, Ahmose-Merytamun, Satamun, Siamun?, Ahmose-Henuttamehu, Ahmose-Tumerisy, Ahmose-Nebetta, Ahmose Sapair. Bottom row, right to left: Ahmose-Nefertari, Ramesses I, Mentjuhotep II, Amenhotep II, Tao II, Ramose?, Ramesses IV, ?, Tuthmosis I.

Princess Ahmose

~𓅓𓇉𓏏𓁐

ms-iaH

born-moon

Mose-Iah

'Born of the Moon'

Father: Seqenenra Tao II

Mother: Queen Sat-Djhuty

Life: Princess Ahmose was a daughter of the Pharaoh Seqenenra Tao II and his sister-wife Sat-Djhuty. She was the half-sister of Pharaoh Ahmose I. Princess Ahmose was given the titles of: 'King's Daughter; King's Sister.'

Death and Burial: She was buried in tomb QV47 in the Valley of the Queens. Her mummy is now in the Egyptian Museum of Turin, Italy.

Prince Ahmose Sapair (Sipair)

MOSE-IAH SA-PA-IR

ms-iaH sA-pA-ir

born-moon son-the-doer

Mose-Iah Sa-Pa-ir

'Born of the Moon, Son the Doer'

Father: Seqenenra Tao II or Ahmose I

Mother: possibly Queen Ahhotep I

Burial: DB320

Life: Prince Ahmose Sapair was probably the son of Seqenenra Tao II and brother of Ahmose I. He appears on several monuments even though he never ascended to the throne.

Death and Burial: His mummy was found in the Deir el Bahri cache (DB320) and was identified as a young six year old boy. The location of his tomb is not known.

Kamose

Ka-mose-nakhet

1555-1550 BC

nsw bit (kA-ms-nxt)

king south, king north (bull-man born-strong)

Nesw Bity (Ka-mose-nakhet)

'King of Upper and Lower Egypt, Man Born of the Strong Bull'

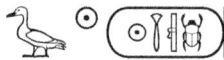

sA ra (wAD-xpr-ra)

son ra (flourishing-manifestations-Ra)

Sa Ra (Wadj-kheper-Ra)

'Son of Ra, Flourishing Manifestations of Ra'

(pa-hqA-qn)

the-prince-brave

Pa-Hekha-qen

'The Brave Prince'

17ᵗʰ Dynasty		New Kingdom 18ᵗʰ Dynasty			
1560 BC	1550 BC	1540 BC	1530 BC	1520 BC	1510 BC
I Tao II Kamose		Ahmose I		Amenhotep I	

Predecessor: Seqenenra Tao II

Successor: Ahmose I

Consort: Ah-hotep II

Children: Ahmose-Satkamose

Father: Seqenenra Tao II

Mother: Ah-hotep I

Died: 1550 BC

Reign: Kamose was the last king of the Theban Seventeenth Dynasty. He was possibly the son of Seqenenra Tao and Ahhotep I and the full brother of Ahmose I, founder of the Eighteenth Dynasty. His reign fell at the very end of the Second Intermediate Period.

He ruled from the south at Thebes while the Hyksos ruled from the north at Avaris. The Theban Seventeenth dynasty rulers were at peace with the Hyksos kingdom to their north prior to the reign of Seqenenra Tao. They controlled Upper Egypt up to Elephantine and ruled Middle Egypt as far north as Kis. Kamose sought to extend his rule northward over all of Lower Egypt. This was met with much opposition by his courtiers. Kamose's records:

'See, all are loyal as far as Kis. We are tranquil in our part of Egypt. Elephantine (at the First Cataract) is strong, and the middle part (of the land) is with us as far as Kis. Men till for us the finest of their lands. Our cattle pasture in the Papyrus marshes. Corn is sent for our swine. Our cattle are not taken away... He holds the land of the Asiatics, we hold Egypt.'

Seqenenra Tao II, his father, had already been engaged in conflict with the Hyksos only to fall in battle. Kamose sought to regain by force what he thought was his by right, namely the kingship of Lower and Upper Egypt:

'I should like to know what serves this strength of mine, when a chieftain in Avaris, and another in Kush, and I sit united with an Asiatic and a Nubian, each in possession of his slice of Egypt, and I cannot pass by him as far as Memphis... No man can settle down, when despoiled by the taxes of the Asiatics. I will grapple with him, that I may rip open his belly! My wish is to save Egypt and to smite the Asiatic!'

In Kamose's third year, he embarked on his military campaign against the Hyksos by sailing north out of Thebes on the Nile. He first reached Neferusy, which was just north of Kis and was manned by an Egyptian garrison loyal to the Hyksos. A detachment of Medjay troops attacked the garrison and overran it.

A second stela found in Thebes, continues Kamose's narrative again with an attack on Avaris. Kamose is known to have campaigned against the Kushites prior to his third year since the Hyksos king directly appeals to his Kushite counterpart to attack his Theban rival and avenge the damage which Kamose had inflicted upon both their states.

Death and Burial: His mummy was moved at some point after burial and was discovered in 1857 at Dra Abu el-Naga, seemingly deliberately hidden in a pile of debris. The painted and stuccoed coffin was uncovered by early Egyptologists, who noted that the mummy was in very poor shape. Buried with the mummy were a gold and silver dagger, amulets, a scarab, a bronze mirror, and a pectoral in the shape of a cartouche bearing the name of his successor and brother, Ahmose I.

Princess Satkamose

SAT-KAMOSE

sAt (ka-mose)

daughter (bull-born)

Sat Ka-mose

'Daughter Born of the Bull'

Spouse: Ahmose I?

Father: ?

Mother: ?

Life: Princess Satkamose was possibly a wife of King Ahmose.

Her titles: 'King's Wife, Great King's Wife, God's Wife, King's Daughter, King's Sister.'

It is not clear where Satkamose fits in the royal family. She may be a daughter of King Kamose based on the fact that her name literally means 'daughter of Kamose'. A statue from Karnak however shows Satkamose as one of the female companions of King Amenhotep I. Ahmose-Nefertari is the other royal woman depicted. Satkamose is given the titles of 'King's Daughter, King's Sister, God's Wife' and this may indicate she was a daughter of King Ahmose and Queen Ahmose-Nefertari. The God's Wife title may be posthumous.

Death and Burial: Satkamose's mummy is known from the Deir el Bahari cache DB 320. She was a relatively tall young woman. She may have been as young as 30 years of age when she died.

Family Tree Dynasty 18: Ahmose I, Amenhotep I and Thutmose I

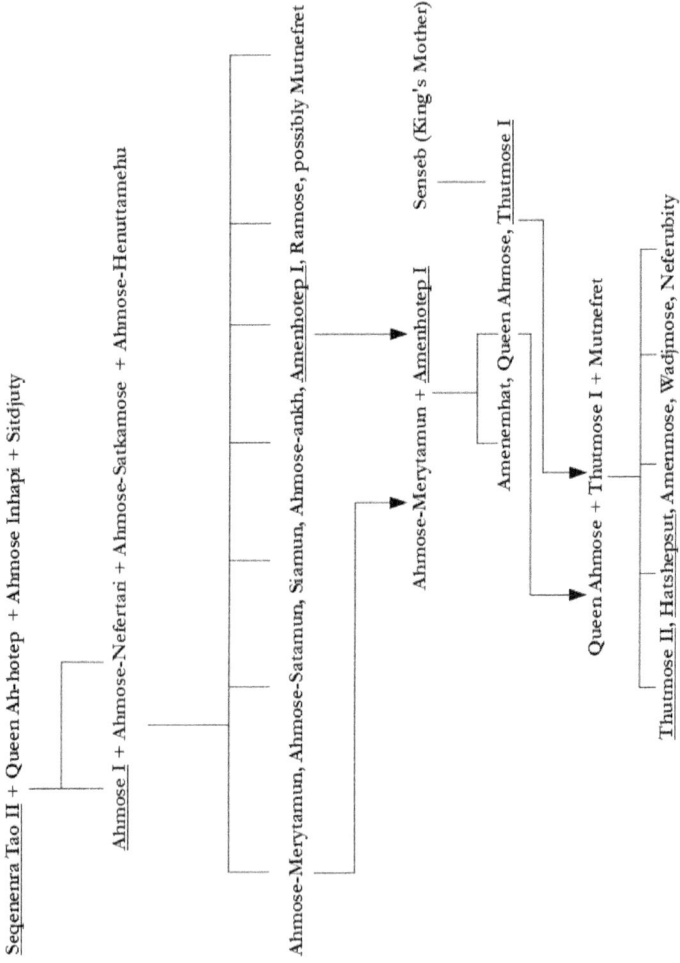

The New Kingdom Period

18th Dynasty

1554-1070 BC

Ahmose I - Nebphetyra

MOSE-IAH NEB-PHETY-RA

1539–1514 BC

Reign: 25 yrs

sa-Ra: ms-s-iaH

Son Ra: born-moon (god Iah)

Sa-Ra Mes-Iah

'Son of Ra: 'Born of the Moon god Iah'

nsw bit: nb-pHty-ra

King South North: lord-strength-Ra

Nsw-Bit: Neb-Phety-Ra

'King of Upper and Lower (Egypt): 'Lord of Strength is Ra'

New Kingdom 18ᵗʰ Dynasty					
1550 BC	1540 BC	1530 BC	1520 BC	1510 BC	1500 BC
Ahmose I			Amenhotep I		Thutmose I

Lived: 12+25 = 37 yrs

Co-regent: his mother Ah-hotep I

Predecessor: Kamose (brother)

Successor: Amenhotep I (his son by Ahmose-Nefertari)

Wives: Ahmose-Nefertari (his sister and God's Wife of Amun), Ahmose-Satkamose, Ahmose-Henuttamehu

Father: Pharaoh Seqenenra Tao II

Mother: Queen Ah-hotep I

Children: Princess Ahmose-Merytamun, Princess Ahmose-Satamun, Prince Siamun, Prince Ahmose-ankh, Amenhotep I, Prince Ramose, possibly Mutnefret

Burial: his tomb is unknown, but his mummy was found in the royal cache of Deir el Bari.

Reign: Pharaoh Ahmose I Nebphetyra was founder of the 18th Dynasty, he overthrew the Hyksos 'Shepherd Kings' of the north at the

44

end of the Second Intermediate Period and re-established rule from Thebes. He was a member of the Theban royal house, the son of Pharaoh Seqenenra Tao II and brother of the last pharaoh of the Seventeenth dynasty, King Kamose. When he was seven his ruling father was killed and at the age of ten or twelve at the mysterious death of his brother, who only ruled for three to five years, he assumed the throne. In Kamose's third year, he embarked on his military campaign against the Hyksos by sailing north out of Thebes on the Nile. After expelling the Hyksos from the north Delta region he successfully reasserted Egyptian power in its formerly subject territories of Nubia and Canaan. He then reorganized the administration of the country, reopened quarries, mines and trade routes and began massive construction projects of a type that had not been undertaken since the time of the Middle Kingdom. This building program culminated in the construction of the last pyramid built by native Egyptian rulers.

Pyramid: the Pyramid of Ahmose I was built not as a tomb, but a cenotaph at the necropolis of Abydos, Egypt. It was the only royal pyramid built in this area. Today only a pile of rubble remains, reaching a height of about 10 m. The pyramid was constructed from sand and rubble and only the usual limestone casing kept the building in shape. It had a base length of 52.5 m (172 ft) and was about 40 m (130 ft) high. The inclination of the sides was 60°.

Queen Ahmose Nefertari

MOSE-IAH NEFER-ITRI

'Woman in Black'

1562-1495 BC

Age: 67 yrs

Nb-TAwy: Ms-IaH-nfr-itry

Lord-Two Lands: born-moon God Iah, Beautiful-Lady

Neb Tawy 'Mose-Iah-Neferitry'

Lord of the Two Lands

'Beautiful Lady, born of the moon god Iah'

Her royal titles depicted in Tomb TT359:

nsw Hmt, nsw Mwt wrt, di anx DtA

King Wife, King Mother Great, Given Life Forever

Nesw Hemet: Nsw Hemet, Nesw Mut Weret, di Ankh Djeta

'King's Great Wife and Mother, Given Life Forever.'

Lived: born 1562 BC and died 1495 BC at the age of 67 years

Spouse: Pharaoh Ahmose I, her brother.

Co-regent: acted as co-regent with her young brother Ahmose I when he succeed the throne and then with her young son Amun-hotep I during his early years.

Father: Pharaoh Seqenenra Tao

Mother: Queen Ah-hotep I who was wife of Seqenenra Tao

Children: Amenhotep I, Ahmose-ankh, Prince Siamun, Ramose ?

Ahmose-Merytamun, Mutnefret? Ahmose-Satamun

Life and Reign: Ahmose Nefertari was 11 years older than her younger brother Ahmose I, who came to be king at the age of 12 at the death of his brother pharaoh Kamose, she married Ahmose her brother becoming his consort queen when she was 23 years of age. She later became co-regent with her son Amenhotep I when her husband died at the age of 37 years, making her at this time 48 years old. She was 56 years old and was the grandmother Tuthmosis I when he came to the throne in 1506 BC.

Ahmose Nefertari's mother, Ah-hotep I, was celebrated as a warrior, since she is shown in her tomb with the 'Golden flies of honour.' Ah-hotep I, helped her sons, Kamose and then Ahmose, to finally drive the Hyksos out of Egypt. Following her mother's actions, Ahmose Nefertari was highly distinguished and helped to reconstruct the country after centuries of foreign rule, principally the Deir el-Medina necropolis. Ahmose Nefertari and her husband, Ahmose I, ruled together for twenty five years. She was lauded on inscriptions throughout Egypt, from Saï to Tura. Her name appears at the alabaster quarries of Asyut and the limestone quarries at Tura:

> 'God's Wife, Great King's Wife, Lady of the Two Lands, King's Daughter, King's Sister, King's Mother, and Princess of the Two Lands.'

Queen Ahmose Nefertari was often depicted with Black Skin; this was nothing to do with her genetic lineage, but to show her as the woman of fertility and regeneration. The colour black being the colour of the fertile valley soil, hence the name for Egypt is Kemet, meaning 'Black Land.'

After her death, Queen Ahmose-Nefertari became a patron deity of the Theban necropolis, alongside her son King Amenhotep I. She was painted on a tomb wall 400 years after she died, when she was being worshipped as a goddess in Thebes.

During her regency with Amenhotep I, they inaugurated the workman's village at Deir el-Medina on the West Bank of the Nile at Luxor. There is a temple at Deir el-Medina dedicated to Amenhotep I known as the 'Lord of the Town' and Ahmose Nefertari, known as the 'Lady of the West' and the 'Mistress of the Sky,' where both were deified by the villagers after their deaths until the late Ramesside period.

Queen Ahmose-Satamun

MOSE-IAH AMUN-SAT

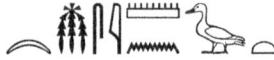

ms-iaH, imn sAt

born-moon, Amun-daughter

Mes-Iah, Amun-sat

'Born of the Moon, Daughter of Amun'

Spouse: Ahmose I

Father: Ahmose I

Brother: Amenhotep I

Life: Satamun was the daughter of Pharaoh Ahmose I and sister of Amenhotep I. A colossal statue of hers stood before the eighth pylon at Karnak. Ahmose-Satamun was a princess of the early Eighteenth dynasty of Egypt. Her mummy was found in the Deir el-Bahari cache (DB320) and is today in the Egyptian Museum, Cairo. Her titles were: 'God's Wife; King's Daughter; King's Sister.'

Queen Ahmose-Henuttamehu

MOSE-IAH-HENUT-TA-MEHU

nsw-sAt (iaH-ms-Hnwt-tA-mHw)

king daughter (moon-born-mistress-Lower Egypt)

Nesw Sat (Mes-Iah-Henut-Ta-Mehu)

'King's Daughter, Moon Born, Mistress of Lower Egypt'

Spouse: Pharaoh Ahmose I

Children: unknown

Father: Seqenenra Tao II

Mother: Ahmose Inhapy

Born: Thebes?

Died: Thebes

Burial: Thebes and then in TT320

Life: Ahmose Henut-ta-mehu 'Child of the Moon; Mistress of Lower Egypt' was a princess and queen of the late 17th to early 18th dynasties of Egypt. Ahmose-Henuttamehu was a daughter of Pharaoh Seqenenra Tao II by his sister-wife Ahmose Inhapy. She was probably married to her half-brother Pharaoh Ahmose I, since her titles include 'King's Wife, Great King's Wife, King's Daughter and King's Sister.' Ahmose-Henuttamehu was a half-sister to the Great Royal Wife and God's Wife of Amun Ahmose-Nefertari. Ahmose Henuttamehu's

51

mummy was discovered in 1881 in her own coffin in the tomb DB320 and is now in the Egyptian Museum in Cairo. Henuttamehu was an old woman when she died, with worn teeth. Quotes from the Book of the Dead were written on her mummy bandages. She was probably buried together with her mother; her mummy was taken to DB320. Ahmose-Henuttamehu is included in the list of royal ancestors worshipped in the Nineteenth Dynasty.

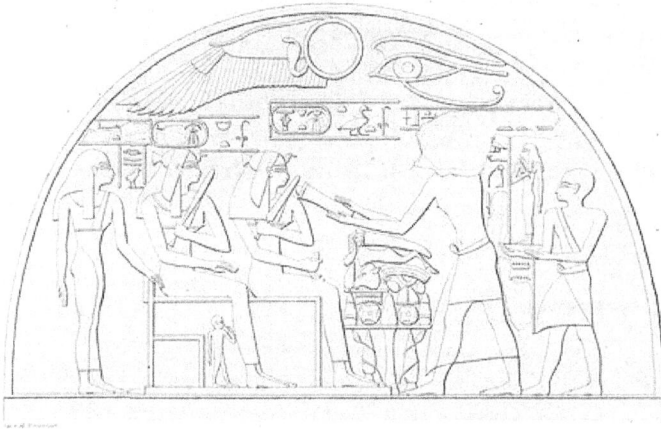

Ahmose-Henuttamehu and possibly her mother Ahmose-Inhapy.

Prince Sa-Amun

SA-AMUN

sa-imn

son-Amun

Sa-Amun

'Son of Amun'

Father: Ahmose I

Mother: Ahmose Nefertari

Life: Sa-Amun was a Prince of ancient Egypt. His name means 'Son of Amun'. Sa-Amun was a prince during the early Eighteenth dynasty and was the son of Pharaoh Ahmose I and Queen Ahmose Nefertari. His mummy was found in the Deir el-Bahari cache (DB320) and is now in the Egyptian Museum in Cairo.

Prince Ahmose-Ankh

MOSE-IAH ANKH

⌒𓅓𓈖𓋹

iaH-ms-anx

Moon-born-Life

Iah-mose-ankh

'Life Born of the Moon'

Father: Pharaoh Ahmose 1

Mother: Queen Ahmose Nefertari

Siblings: Princess Ahmose-Merytamun, Princess Ahmose-Satamun, Prince Sa-Amun, Amenhotep I, Prince Ramose, possibly Mutnefret

Life: Prince Ahmose-ankh was a prince during the early Eighteenth dynasty of Egypt and was the son of Pharaoh Ahmose I and Queen Ahmose Nefertari. He was the crown prince but pre-deceased his father, thus the next pharaoh was his younger brother Amenhotep I. His sister was Ahmose-Merytamun.

A stela which depicts him with his parents is now in the Luxor Museum.

Prince Ramose

𓇳𓅭𓏥𓏤

ms-ra

born-Moon

Mose-Ra

'Born of Ra'

Father: Pharaoh Ahmose I

Life: Ramose was an ancient Egyptian prince of the eighteenth dynasty; probably the son of Pharaoh Ahmose I.

He is depicted in the 20th dynasty tomb of Inherkhau (TT359) among the 'Lords of the West' with several of his family members and a few important pharaohs, among the depicted are (Amenhotep I, Ahmose I, Ahhotep, Ahmose Merytamun, Ahmose Satamun, Sa-Amun, Ahmose Henuttamehu, Ahmose Tumerisy, Ahmose Nebetta, Ahmose Sapair, Ahmose Nefertari, Ramesses I, Mentjuhotep II, Amenhotep II, Seqenenra Tao II, Ramesses IV, Thutmose I. A statue of his is owned by the University of Liverpool.

The tomb of Inherkhau TT359: the bottom register shows the deceased, Inherkhau seated before the Sem Priest dressed in a leopard's skin:

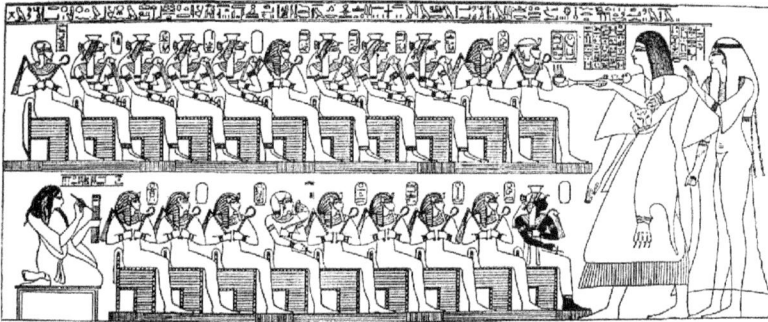

The south-east wall in the tomb of Inherkhau showing the deceased and his wife present themselves facing twenty royal divinities, distributed on two registers, in front of which Inherkhau carries out the fumigation with the help of a long censer. On the top row are three kings and seven queens. The first two are Amen-hotep I and Ahmose I, respectively second and first king of the 18th Dynasty. The last character is the prince Sa-pa-iry who is distinguishable by the absence of a cartouche and uraeus; he has the lock of hair worn by royal children and a short beard.

The lower row consists of seven kings, a prince and queen Ahmose Nefertari, represented with black flesh, together with her son, Amenhotep I.

Amenhotep I - Djeserkara

HOTEP-AMUN DJSER-KA-RA

1526-1506 BC

Reigned 20 yrs

sA-ra (Htp-imn)

son Ra (Hotep-Amun)

Sa Ra: Hotep-Amun

Son of Ra: 'Satisfied is Amun'

nsw bit (Dsr-kA-ra)

Sedge Bee (sacred-ka-ra)

Nsw Bit (Djser-ka-ra)

King of the South and North 'Sacred Soul of Ra'

New Kingdom 18ᵗʰ Dynasty						
1550 BC	1540 BC	1530 BC	1520 BC	1510 BC	1500 BC	
	Ahmose I			Amenhotep I		Thutmose I

Predecessor: Ahmose I

Successor: Thutmose I

Consort: Ahmose Merytamun, Satkamose, Queen Senseneb?

Father: Ahmose I

Mother: Ahmose Nefertari

Children: Amenemhat (died young), Thutmose I?

Died: 1506 0r 1504 BC

Burial: Mummy found in Deir el Bahri cache, originally buried in Dra Abu el Naga or KV39

Family tree:

Ahmose-Merytamun + <u>Amenhotep I</u>   Senseb (King's Mother)

Amenemhat, Queen Ahmose, <u>Thutmose I</u>

Queen Ahmose + <u>Thutmose I</u> + Mutnefret

<u>Thutmose II</u>, <u>Hatshepsut</u>, Amenmose, Wadjmose, Neferubity

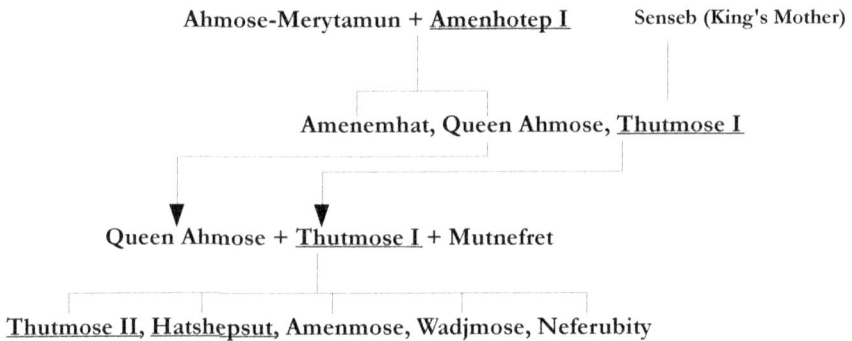

Reign: Amenhotep I was the son of Ahmose I and Queen Ahmose Nefertari, he co-reigned with his mother and both were later worshipped as gods. He was the second pharaoh of the 18t Dynasty. He had at least two elder brothers, Ahmose-ankh and Ahmose Sa-pa-ir, and was not expected to inherit the throne. His elder brother Ahmose-ankh was crown-prince and heir apparent to the throne of their father

Ahmose I, but the crown prince and his other elder brother died before their father's reign ended, and so Amenhotep I became crown prince. Amenhotep I and his mother Ahmose Nefertari are credited with founding a settlement for workers in the Theban Necropolis at Deir el-Medina. Amenhotep I took his sister Ahmose-Merytamun as his Great Royal Wife. Another wife's name, Satkamose, is attested on a nineteenth dynasty stele.

Amenhotep I left few records about his 20 year reign, according to Ahmose, son of Ebana, Amenhotep I led a military expedition to Kush, where:

'Then I conveyed King Djser-ka-ra, the justified, when he sailed south to Kush, to enlarge the borders of Egypt. His majesty smote that Nubian Bowman in the midst of his army. They were carried off in fetters, none missing, the fleeing destroyed as if they had never been. Now I was in the van of our troops and I fought really well. His majesty saw my valour. I carried off two hands and presented them to his majesty. Then his people and his cattle were pursued, and I carried off a living captive and presented him to his majesty. I brought his majesty back to Egypt in two days from 'Upper Well,' and was rewarded with gold. I brought back two female slaves as booty, apart from those that I had presented to his majesty. Then they made me a 'Warrior of the Ruler."

Amenhotep I began or continued a number of building projects at temple sites in Upper Egypt but most of structures he built were later dismantled or obliterated by his successors. From written sources it is known that he commissioned the architect Ineni to expand the Temple of Karnak. Ineni's tomb biography indicates that he created a 20 cubit gate of limestone on the south side of Karnak. He constructed a sacred barque chapel of Amun out of alabaster and a copy of the White Chapel of Senwasret III.

Stela showing Amenhotep I with his mother Ahmose Nefertari

Queen Ahmose Merytamun

IAH-MOSE MERYT-AMUN

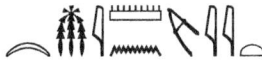

ms-iaH mryt-Imn

born-moon beloved Amun

Iah-Mose-Meryt-Amun

'Born of the Moon, Beloved of Amun'

Spouse: Amenhotep I

Father: Pharaoh Ahmose I

Mother: Queen Ahmose Nefertari

Burial: TT358 in Thebes

Life: Ahmose-Merytamun was a Queen of Egypt during the early Eighteenth dynasty of Egypt. She was both the sister and the wife of Pharaoh Amenhotep I. She died fairly young and was buried in tomb TT358 in Deir el-Bahari. Ahmose-Merytamun was the royal daughter of Ahmose I and Ahmose Nefertari, and became the Great Royal Wife of her brother Amenhotep I,

Merytamun took over the very important title of 'God's Wife of Amun' 🞜🞜🞜 Hemet-Netjer-en-Amun, from her mother Ahmose Nefertari. God's Wife of Amun was the highest-ranking priestess of the Amun cult (see Appendix #4). Other titles recorded for Merytamun include: 'Lady of the Two Lands, King's Great Wife, Mistress of the Two Lands, God's Wife, United with the White Crown, King's Daughter, and King's Sister.'

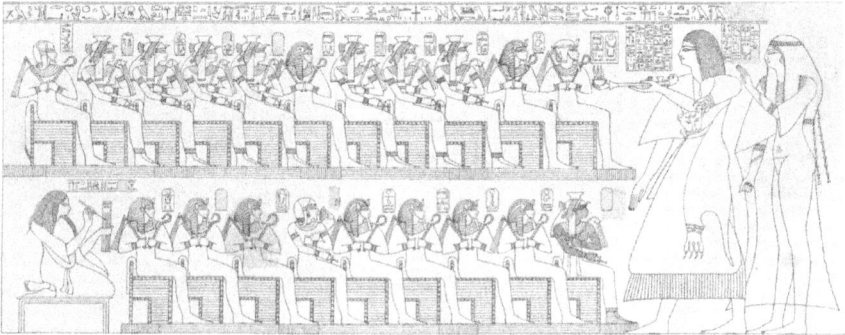

The above scene is from the tomb of Inherkhau dating to the Twentieth dynasty of Egypt. Top row, right to left: Amenhotep I, Ahmose I, Ahhotep I, Ahmose-Merytamun, Satamun, Siamun?, Ahmose-Henuttamehu, Ahmose-Tumerisy, Ahmose-Nebetta, Ahmose Sapair. Bottom row, right to left: Ahmose-Nefertari, Ramesses I, Mentjuhotep II, Amenhotep II, Tao II, Ramose?, Ramesses IV, ?, Tuthmosis I.

Death and Burial: Her remains were discovered at Deir el-Bahri in TT358 in 1930 by Winlock. Her mummy was found in two cedar wood coffins and a cartonage outer case. It had been rewrapped and reburied by priests who had found her tomb that had been vandalized by robbers. It appears that she died when she was relatively young, with evidence of being afflicted with arthritis and scoliosis.

Queen Senseneb

Queen Senseneb was the mother of Pharaoh Thutmose I of the early New Kingdom. She bore the title of King's Mother and is thought to have been a commoner. Senseneb is depicted on painted reliefs from the Mortuary Temple of Hatshepsut at Deir el-Bahri. Te text reads:

[nswt] bity [mwt nswt] Hnwt tAwy (sn-snb) anx Dd DtA

? bity? mistress two-lands (Sen-seneb) life stability forever

'Mistress of the Two Lands, Senseneb, Life Forever'

MOSE-DJHWTY

1506-1493 BC

Reigned 13 yrs

sA-ra (ms-DHwty)

son Ra (born-Djhwty)

Sa Ra (Mose-Djhwty)

'Son of Ra, Born of Djhwty (Ibis god)

nsw bit (aA-xpr-kA-ra)

King Upper Lower Egypt (great-creation-soul-Ra)

Nsw Bit (Aa-kheper-ka-Ra)

'King of Upper and Lower Egypt, Great Manifestation of the Ka of Ra'

sA-ra (ms-DHwty-s-xa-mi-ra)

son Ra (born-Djhwty-appearing-like-Ra)

Sa Ra (Mose-Djhwty, S-kha-mi-Ra)

'Son of Ra, Born of Djhwty, Appearing like Ra'

New Kingdom 18th Dynasty						
1550 BC	1540 BC	1530 BC	1520 BC	1510 BC	1500 BC	1490 BC
Ahmose I			Amenhotep I		Thutmose I	Thutmose II

Consort: Queen Ahmose (mother of Hatshepsut), Mutnefret

Father: Unknown, possibly Amenhotep I by Queen Senseneb

Mother: Queen Senseneb

Children: Thutmose II, Hatshepsut, Amenmose, Wadjmose, Nererubity

Died: 1493 BC

Burial: KV38, later KV20

Monuments: Pylons IV and V, two obelisks and a hypostyle hall at Karnak

Family tree:

Ahmose-Merytamun + <u>Amenhotep I</u>   Senseb (King's Mother)

Amenemhat, Queen Ahmose, <u>Thutmose I</u>

Queen Ahmose + <u>Thutmose I</u> + Mutnefret

<u>Thutmose II</u>, <u>Hatshepsut</u>, Amenmose, Wadjmose, Neferubity

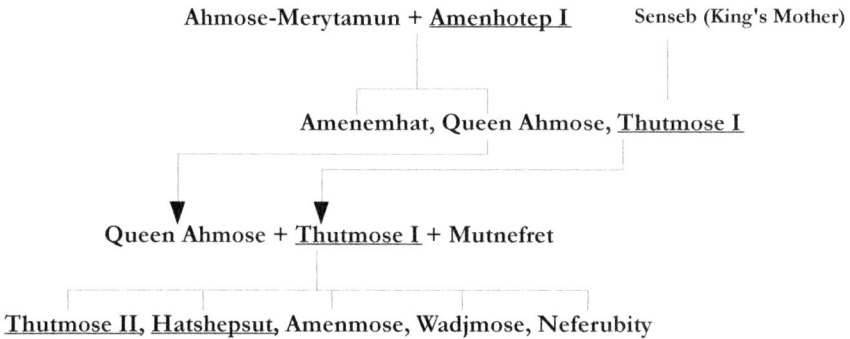

Reign: Thutmose I was possibly the son of Amenhotep I and Queen Senseneb.   He married his half-sister Princess Ahmose, who was possibly the daughter of Queen Ah-hotep, or the daughter of Ahmose I and Queen Ahmose Nefertari, whichever is true he did it in order to secure the throne.   Thutmose I and is wife Queen Ahmose were the parents of the infamous Queen Hatshepsut.

Prince Amenmose, Thutmose's first-born son, probably by his wife Ahmose, eventually became the 'great army-commander of his father.' Prince Amenmose predeceased his father. Thutmose had another son, Wadjmose, and two daughters, Hatshepsut and Neferu-bity, by Ahmose. Wadjmose died before his father, and Neferu-bity died as an infant. Thutmose I had one son by another wife, Mutnefret. This son succeeded him as Thutmose II, whom Thutmose I married to his daughter, Hatshepsut.

Although Thutmose I had a short reign, he embarked upon a series of brilliant military campaigns that set the seal for the glory of the 18th Dynasty.

Ahmose, son of Ebana records:

'Then I conveyed King Aa-kheper-ka-ra (Thutmose I), the justified, when he sailed south to Khent-hen-nefer (𓈉 ⌢ 𓉾𓃀𓂻 Nubia), to crush rebellion throughout the lands, to repel the intruders from the desert region. I was brave in his presence in the bad water, in the towing of the ship over the cataract. Thereupon I was made crew commander. Then his majesty [was informed that the Nubian] ... At this his majesty became enraged like a leopard. His majesty shot, and his first arrow pierced the chest of that foe. Then those [enemies turned to flee], helpless before his Uraeus. A slaughter was made among them; their dependents were carried off as living captives. His majesty journeyed north, all foreign lands in his grasp, and that wretched Nubian Bowman head downward at the bow of his majesty's ship 'Falcon.' They landed at Ipet-sut.'

Ipet-sut: 'The Most Selected of Places,' was the area around Karnak and the main place of worship of the eighteenth dynasty Theban Triad with the god Amun as its head. It is part of the monumental city of Thebes.

After that campaign, he led a second expedition against Nubia in his third year in the course of which he ordered the canal at the first cataract, which had been built under Senwasret III of the 12th Dynasty, to be dredged in order to facilitate easier travel upstream from Egypt to Nubia. This helped integrate Nubia into the Egyptian empire. This expedition is mentioned in two separate inscriptions by the king's son Thure:

'Year 3, first month of the third season, day 22, under the majesty of the King of Upper and Lower Egypt, Aakheperkara who is given life. His Majesty commanded to dig this canal after he found it stopped up with stones so that no ship sailed upon it.'

'Year 3, first month of the third season, day 22. His Majesty sailed this canal in victory and in the power of his return from overthrowing the wretched Kush.'

The Syrian campaign of Thutmose I recorded by Ahmose, son of Ebana:

'After this (his majesty) proceeded to Retjenu (Northern Canaan), to vent his wrath throughout the lands. When his majesty reached Nahrin, (Eastern Mesopotamia, i.e. the land between the two rivers) his majesty found that foe marshalling troops. Then his majesty made a great slaughter of them. Countless were the living captives which his majesty brought back from his victories. Now I was in the van of our troops, and his majesty saw my valour. I brought a chariot, its horse, and him who was on it as a living captive. When they were presented to his majesty, I was rewarded with gold once again.'

Death and Burial: Thutmose I was originally buried and then reburied in KV20 in a double burial with his daughter Hatshepsut. Howard Carter discovered 2 separate coffins in the burial chamber. The beautifully carved sarcophagus of Hatshepsut 'was discovered open with no sign of a body, and with the lid lying discarded on the floor.' A second sarcophagus was found lying on its side with its almost undamaged lid propped against the wall nearby. This second quartzite sarcophagus had originally been engraved with the name of 'the King of Upper and Lower Egypt, Maatkare Hatshepsut.' It bears a dedication text which records Hatshepsut's generosity towards her father:

"...long live the Female Horus...The king of Upper and Lower Egypt, Maatkare, the son of Re, Hatshepsut-Khenemet-Amun! May she live forever! She made it as her monument to her father whom she loved, the Good God, Lord of the Two Lands, Aakheperkare, the son of Re, Thutmosis the justified.'

Queen Ahmose

QUEEN MOSE-IAH

iaH-ms

Moon-born

Mes-Iah

'Born of the Moon'

Spouse: Pharaoh Thutmose I

Children: Hatshepsut, Princess Nefer-bity

Father: unknown

Mother: Unknown

Born: possibly Thebes or the north

Died: probably when she was young

Burial: unknown

Life: Queen Ahmose was the Great Royal Wife of the dynasty's third pharaoh, Thutmose I, and the mother of the queen and pharaoh Hatshepsut. Her name means 'Born of the Moon'.

It is not known who Queen Ahmose's father and mother were. It has been suggested that Ahmose was either a daughter of pharaoh Amenhotep I or a daughter of pharaoh Ahmose I and possibly Ahmose I's sister-wife Ahmose-Nefertari. Her title 'King's Sister' suggests that she may have been the sister of her husband pharaoh Thutmose I. Her other titles included:

'Hereditary Princess, Great of Praises, Mistress of Great Beloved Sweetness, Great King's Wife, his beloved, Mistress of Joy, Lady of all Women, Mistress of the Two Lands, Companion of Horus, Beloved Companion of Horus, King's Sister.'

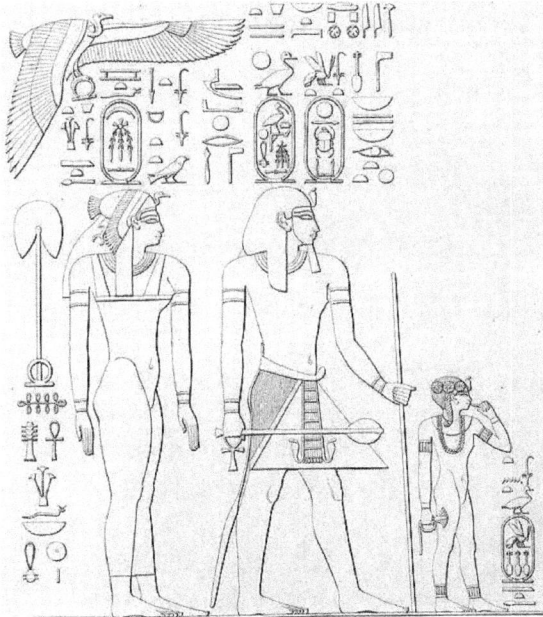

Pharaoh Thutmose I of the 18th dynasty of Ancient Egypt, with his chief wife Queen Ahmose and daughter Neferu-bity, the father, mother and sister of Hatshepsut.

The inscription gives the king's titles:

'The Good God, Lord of the Two Lands, Lord of Doing Things, King of the South and the North, Aa-kheper-ka-Ra, Son of Ra, Mose-Djhuty Like Ra, True of Voice, the Great God.'

Above the queen is her name and titles:

71

nswt snt, nsw Hmt wrt, mryt.f (Iah-ms) Hnwt Smaw-mHw, mAa-xrw

king's sister, king's wife great, beloved.of him (Iah-Mose) mistress
south north, justified

**'The King's Sister and Great Wife, Iah-mose, Mistress of the
South and the North, True-of-Voice.'**

Their daughter has the titles:

nswt sAt (bity-nfrw) mAa xrw

King's Daughter, Neferu-bity, mAa-xrw

'King's Daughter, Neferu-bity (Northern Beauty), True of Voice.'

Nefer-bity was the daughter of Pharaoh Thutmose I and Ahmose, the
sister of Hatshepsut and the half-sister of Thutmose II, Wadjmose and
Amenmose.

She is depicted with her parents in Hatshepsut's Deir el-Bahari
mortuary temple, she then vanishes from record. It is assumed that she
died young.

Prince Amenmose

AMEN-MOSE

nswt sA, imn-ms

king's son, Amun-mose

Neswt Sa, Imun-mose

'King's Son, Born of Amun'

Father: Thutmose I

Mother: Ahmose? Mutnefret?

Life: Amenmose was an Ancient Egyptian prince. He lived during the 18th dynasty and was the eldest son and designated heir of Thutmose I, but he predeceased his father. It is not known who was his mother or his brother Wadjmose's mother. She is likely to have been either the Great Royal Wife Ahmose, who was also the mother of Hatshepsut and Neferu-bity, or the secondary queen Mutnefret, who also was the mother of Thutmose II

Amenmose was the first Egyptian prince to receive a military title, that of 'Great Overseer of Soldiers.' He was the first prince to have is name written in a royal cartouche.

Amenmose with his brother Wadjmose in the el-Kab tomb of their tutor, Paheri.

The inscription reads:

irt nsw di Htp in nswt sA wAD-ms sn.f mry.f nswt sA Imn-ms

made king's offering by king's son, Wadj-mose,

brother.his, king's son, Amen-mose

Irt Nesw di hetep, in Neswt Sa, Wadj-mose, sen.ef meryt.ef, Neswt Sa Imen-mose

'A king's offering made by the king's son, Wadj-mose, and his brother, the king's son, Amen-mose.'

Prince Wadjmose

WADJ-MOSE

nswt sA, wAD-ms

king's son, Wadj-mose

Nswt Sa, Wadj-mose

'King's Son, Born of Vigour'

Father: Thutmose I

Mother: ?

Life: Prince Wadjmose had a brother named Amenmose; it is not known who their mother was. If they were born to Queen Ahmose, they were full brothers of Hatshepsut and Neferu-bity. Wadjmose may have been the son of Queen Mutnefret and thus a full brother of Thutmose II. Wadjmose's name occurs written in a cartouche, which is quite rare for princes.

Wadjmose is depicted in the El-Kab tomb of his and Amenmose's tutor Pa-hery, as sitting on Pa-hery's lap. He is thought to have predeceased his father.

Prince Wadjmose seated on the lap of his tutor Pa-hery

The inscription above his head gives the titles of Wadjmose and Pa-hery:

nsw sA, wAD-ms, HAty-a n nxb (Nekheb), pA-Hry mAa-xrw

king's son, Wadj-mose, governor of Nekheb, the chief, true-voice

Nesw Sa, Wadj-mose, Haty-a en Nekheb, Pa-Hery, Maa-kheru

'The King's Son, Born of Vigour, Governor of ancient Nekhen (el-Kab), Pa-hery (the Chief), True of Voice (Justified).'

Queen Mutnefret

MUT-NEFERET

mwt-nfrt

mother-beautiful

Mut-nefret

'The Beautiful Goddess, Mut'

Spouse: Thutmose I

Father: Ahmose I?

Mother: ?

Life: Queen Mutnefret was a secondary wife of Thutmose I and the mother of Thutmose II. Based on her titles of King's Daughter and King's Sister, she is likely to have been a daughter of Ahmose I and a sister of Amenhotep I.

She was probably the mother of Thutmose I's other sons, Amenmose, Wadjmose and Ramose.

Queen Mutnefret was depicted in the Deir el-Bahri temple built by her grandson Thutmose III, on a stela found at the Ramesseum, on the colossus of her son, and a statue of her, bearing a dedication by Thutmose II, was found in Wadjmose's chapel.

Thutmose II- Aakheperenra

MOSE-DJHWTY

1493-1479 BC or 1513-1499 BC

Reign: 14 yrs, possibly only 3 years

sA ra (ms-DHwty)

son Ra (born-Djhuty (Ibis god))

Sa Ra (Mose-Djhuty)

'Son of Ra, Born of Djhuty'

nsw bit (aA-xpr-n-ra)

king-south king-north (great-manifestation-of-Ra)

Nesw Bity (Aa-kheper-en-Ra)

'King of the South and the North,

Great is the Manifestation of Ra'

sA-ra (ms-DHwty, nfr-xAw)

son Ra (born-Djhuty, good-appearances)

Sa Ra, Mose-Djhuty, Nefer-Khaw

'Son of Ra, Born of Djhwty, Perfect in Appearance'

1530 BC	1520 BC	1510 BC	1500 BC	1490 BC	1490 BC	1490 BC
Amenhotep I		Thutmose I		Thutmose II		Hatshepsut

Consort: his half-sister Queen Hatshepsut, secondary wife Queen Iset

Father: Pharaoh Thutmose I

Mother: Queen Mutnefret

Children: Pharaoh Thutmose III, Princess Neferura

Died: 1479 BC

Burial: KV42?

Reign: Pharaoh Thutmose II was the son of Thutmose I and is minor wife Queen Mutnefret. He married his half-sister Queen Hatshepsut, who was of the same father, but different mother, the Great Royal Wife of Thutmose I, Queen Ahmose:

GRW Queen Ahmose + **Thutmose I** + Concubine Queen Mutnefret

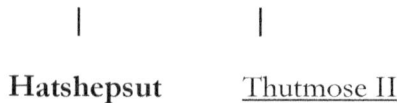

| |

Hatshepsut   Thutmose II

It can be seen from the above, that Hatshepsut, although female had the strongest blood line, thus Thutmose II chose to marry his fully

80

royal half-sister to secure his claim to the throne. Hatshepsut claimed to be her father's chosen heir.

Thutmose II fathered Neferura with Hatshepsut, but also managed to father a male heir, the famous Thutmose III, by a lesser wife named Iset, before his death:

GRW Queen Ahmose + **Thutmose I** + Concubine Queen Mutnefret

| |

Hatshepsut + Thutmose II + Iset

| |

Princess Neferura   Thutmose III

Although during the reign of Thutmose II military campaigns were carried out in Nubia, the Levant* and the Shasu Bedouin in the Sinai, these campaigns were carried out by his generals and not by the king himself, probably because he was still a minor with his half-sister Hatshepsut acting as co-regent. Hatshepsut may have been the real power behind the throne during the short reign (13 or 3 years) of Thutmose II, for later during the rule of his successor, Thutmose III, she crowned herself Pharaoh.

*The Levant in ancient Egyptian was called: Retjenu: 𓏭𓊖𓂋𓈖𓏤 and referred to Syria and Canaan.

Death and Burial: Thutmose II's mummy was discovered in the cache of royal mummies found at Deir el Bahri.

Queen Iset

ASET

ﾘﾚ

Ast

Aset (Iset, Isis)

Spouse: Thutmose II

Father: ?

Mother: ?

Children: Thutmose III

Burial: Thebes?

Life: Iset (Aset, Isis) was the secondary wife or concubine of Thutmose II and the mother of Thutmose III.

When her husband Thutmose II died in 1479 BC, Hatshepsut, the Great Royal Wife, became regent for her young son Thutmose III. Hatshepsut then ruled as Pharaoh until her death when her co-regent, Thutmose III, became Pharaoh. At that time, Iset was given the title of 'King's Mother (to Thutmose III).'

Iset is depicted by her son Thutmose III several times in his tomb in KV34.

Death and Burial: mummy found in Deir el Bahri mummy cache DB320.

Queen Iset standing behind her son Thutmose III

The inscription reads:

a) Thutmose III titles and cartouche:

nswt bity nb irt xt (mn-xpr-ra) di anx

king- south-north lord doing things (established-manifestations-Ra)

given life

Neswt Bity Neb Iret Xet (Men-kheper-Ra) di Ankh

**'King of Upper and Lower Egypt, Lord of Doing Things, Established
are the Manifestations of Ra, given Life'**

b) Queen Iset's titles and cartouche:

nsw Hmt wrt, mryt.f, Hnwt Smaw mHw (Ast) anx DtA

king wife great, beloved.his, mistress south north (Isis) life forever

Nesw Hemet Weret, Meryt.ef, Henut Shemau Mehu

(Iset) Ankh Djeta

'King's Great Wife, Mistress of the South and the North,

Isis, given Life forever.'

KHENUMT-IMUN-HAT-SHEPSUT

MAAT-KA-RA

1479-1458 BC

Co-regent 14 yrs, Reign: 22 yrs

sA ra (Xnmt-imn-HAt-Sps)

son Ra (united-Imun-foremost-noble ladies)

Sa Ra (Khenumt-Imun-Hat-Shepsut)

'Son of Ra, United with Amun, Foremost of Noble Ladies'

nswt bity (mAat-kA-ra)

king-south-north (true-soul-Ra)

Neswt Bity (Maat-ka-Ra)

'King of the South and North, Truth is the Soul of Ra'

1490 BC	1480 BC	1470 BC	1460 BC	1450 BC	1440 BC	1430 BC

Thutmose II   Hatshepsut

Thutmose III

Predecessor: Thutmose II, her half-brother

Successor: Thutmose III, her nephew

Consort: Thutmose II, her younger half-brother

Children: Princess Neferu-ra

Father: Thutmose I

Mother: Great Royal Wife, Queen Ahmose.

Reign: Hatshepsut was the daughter of Thutmose I and Queen Ahmose. She may have co-reigned with her father and with her half-brother Thutmose II. She seized the throne from her nephew Thutmose III and later co-reigned with him.

By year 2 of her co-regency with her young nephew, the child king Thutmose III, she had already begun her policy to subvert his position. Early reliefs show her standing behind Thutmose III with the titles 'Great King's Wife' of Thutmose II. This changed as she gathered support from high officials and it was not long before she began to build a splendid mortuary temple at Deir el Bahri.

The mortuary temple of Hatshepsut at Deir el Bahri was constructed under the supervision of her steward Senenmut it was built of limestone with three colonnade-fronted terraces. The temple was dedicated to the god Amun, with smaller shrines to the goddess Hathor. There is a central rock cut sanctuary on the upper terrace. She claimed it had been built 'as a garden for my father Amun.' All of her propaganda, including her conception by the god Amun and her mother, Queen Ahmose, was to emphasise that she had been deliberately chosen, not just by her father Thutmose I, but by the god Amun to be the next king.

In order to strengthen her position as Pharaoh and King of Egypt she took on the titles of the female Horus Wasretkau 'King of Upper and Lower Egypt,' Maat-ka-Ra and Khenemet Amun Hatshepsut:

Hr [wsr-t-kAw] **Horus: Wasret-kau** 'Mighty of Kas'

nswt bity (**Maat-ka-Ra**) 'Truth is the Ka of Ra'

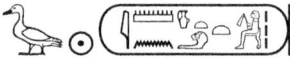

sA-ra xnmt-HAt-Spswt 'Son of Ra, United with Amun, Foremost of Noble Ladies.'

As king she portrayed herself with the king's regalia, including the royal false beard.

Hatshepsut's Obelisks: Queen Hatshepsut erected four obelisks in the temple of Amun at Karnak, two of which have disappeared. Of the remaining pair, the northern one still stands, the other has fallen. The obelisks are made of pink Aswan granite and are cut from one solid block of stone. The obelisk stands 97.5 feet high and estimates of its weight vary from 320 to 700 tons, an inscription at its base records that it took seven months of labour to cut the monolith out of the quarry.

The obelisks were erected to the glory of Amun and to the memory of her father Thutmose I. She states in the inscription that the gilding of the obelisk required large amounts of the finest gold, electrum (gold with a high silver content which was more prized than pure gold).

Shaft inscription:

'...Wrought with very fine electrum, they illuminate the two lands like Aten. Never was the like made since earth's beginning...'

Base inscription:

'...the making for him (Amun) of two great obelisks of hard granite of the South, their upper side (surface) being of electrum, of the best of all foreign lands. Seen on both sides of the river, their rays flood the Two Lands when Aten (the sun) dawns between them, as he rises in heaven's light-land.'

Expedition to Punt: is recorded on the walls of her temple. It shows the envoys setting off down the Red Sea and their arrival at Punt, where they exchange goods and acquire fragrant incense trees.

Hatshepsut reigned for almost 22 years. According to Josephus her reign is given as twenty-one years and nine months, while Africanus gives twenty-two years. At this point in the histories, records of the reign of Hatshepsut end, since the first major foreign campaign of Thutmose III was dated to his twenty-second year, which also would have been Hatshepsut's twenty-second year as pharaoh:

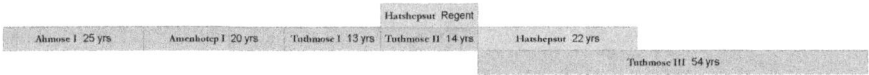

			Hatshepsut Regent		
Ahmose I 25 yrs	Amenhotep I 20 yrs	Tuthmose I 13 yrs	Tuthmose II 14 yrs	Hatshepsut 22 yrs	
					Tuthmose III 54 yrs

Death and Burial: Hatshepsut died when she was middle aged in her twenty second regnal year. Her tomb is in the Valley of the Kings, KV20, but her mummy has not properly been identified.

Princess Neferura

NEFER-U-RA

1473-1462/57 BC

Lived 11/16 yrs

nfr-w-ra

beauty-Ra

Nefer-u-Ra

'The Beauty of Ra'

Father: Pharaoh Thutmose II

Mother: Queen Hatshepsut

Tutor: Senenmut

Life: Princess Neferura was the daughter of two pharaohs, Hatshepsut and Thutmose II. She served in high offices in the government and the religious administration of Ancient Egypt. She was the only child by Thutmose II through his wife Hatshepsut; she lived 11/16 years.

Pharaoh Thutmose III, born of her father and a minor queen, Iset, was her half-brother. Neferura was tutored by Hatshepsut's trusted advisors:

Tutor Ahmose Pen Nekhebet: was an ancient Egyptian official who started his career under Ahmose I and served all the pharaohs until Thutmose III. He held many offices such as wearer of the royal seal, chief treasurer and herald. He was the first tutor of Neferura, daughter of Hatshepsut. In his tomb he writes:

'For me the god's wife repeated favours, the king's great wife Maatkare justified; I brought up her eldest (daughter), the princess Neferura, justified, while she was (still) a child at the breast.'

Tutor Senenmut: was depicted in many statues with Neferura, one statue shows Neferura seated on his lap, the statue bears his and her titles:

imy-r pr, n nsw sAt (nfr-w-ra) sn-n-mwt

overseer house, of king daughter (Beautiful Ra) brother-(of)-mother

Imir Per en Nesw Sat (Nefer-u-Ra) Sen-en-mut

'Over-seer of the House (steward) of the King's Daughter, Neferura (Beautiful-is-Ra), Senenmut (Mother's-Brother)'

When her mother Hatshepsut, took control of the throne, Neferura became more prominent at royal court and was given the titles: 'Lady of Upper and Lower Egypt, Mistress of the Lands.' She also fulfilled the ritual duties required of 'God's Wife of Amun' at the Temple of Karnak. Neferura may have lived after her mother's death and because of her royal genealogy and title of 'God's wife of Amun' married her half-brother Thutmose III and given birth to his eldest son Amenemhat. There is evidence that during this time she was given the titles: 'Great Royal Wife' and 'God's Wife.'

Burial: A tomb (Wady C of the Wady Gabbanat el-Qurud Valley of the Monkeys) which may have been intended for her was discovered by Howard Carter.

Family Tree: Hatshepsut, Thutmose II

Senseb (King's Mother)

Ahmose-Merytamun + Amenhotep I

Amenemhat, Queen Ahmose, Thutmose I

Thutmose I + Mutnefret

Queen Ahmose + Thutmose I

Thutmose II, Hatshepsut, Amenmose, Wadjmose, Neferubity

Thutmose II + Queen Iset

Thutmose III

Thutmose II + Hatshepsut

Neferura

MOSE-DJHWTY

1479-1425 BC

Reign 54 yrs

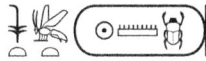

nswt bity (mn-xpr-ra)

king-south-north (established-manifestations-Ra)

Neswt-Bity (Men-kheper-Ra)

'King of Egypt, Enduring Manifestations of Ra'

sA ra (ms-DHwty, nfr-xpr)

son Ra (born-Djhuty, good-created forms)

Sa Ra (Mose-Djhuty, Nefer-kheper)

'Son of Ra (Born of Djhuty, Beautiful of Forms'

1480 BC	1470 BC	1460 BC	1450 BC	1440 BC	1430 BC	1420 BC	1410 BC	1400 BC
	Hatshepsut						Amenhotep II	
			Thutmose III					

Consort: Satiah, Hatshepsut Merytra, Nebtu, Menwi, Merti Menhet, Nebsemi

Father: Thutmose II

Mother: Iset

Children: Prince Amenemhat, Amenhotep II, Baketamun, Iset, Menkheperra, Merytamun, Merytamun, Nebetiunet, Nefertiry, Siamun

Born: 1481 BC

Died: 1425 BC

Burial: KV34

Reign: Thutmose III was the son of Thutmose II. He succeeded to the throne when he was nine years old, but his stepmother and aunt, Hatshepsut, seized royal power and declared herself king and so he co-reigned with her for the first twenty two years of his reign. When Hatshepsut died in year 22 of his reign, he became sole ruler of Egypt.

Because of the prowess he later demonstrated on the battlefield, during his early years of reign under Hatshepsut, he must have spent time training and learning the skills of war with his army. After her death and his later rise to pharaoh of the kingdom, he created the largest empire Egypt had ever seen; no fewer than seventeen campaigns were conducted, and he conquered from Niya in North Syria to the Fourth Cataract of the Nile in Nubia. Nearly 350 cities were captured during his reign, all over the areas of the Near East, Nubia and Euphrates. He made seventeen military campaigns, and used warfare as a way of turning Egypt into a superpower and a military force to be reckoned with. Thutmose III is considered to be one of Egypt's greatest warrior pharaohs.

One of Thutmose III's greatest achievements was the defeat of a large group of Canaanites at the Battle of Megiddo. After the death of Hatshepsut, the Canaanites with the help of the kings of Kadesh and Megiddo revolted and in response Thutmose III mounted a military campaign. The main reason for keeping Egyptian control was the fact Megiddo stood in a prime position in terms of trade routes. Without Megiddo open to Egyptian trade, it would have been very damaging to Egyptian economy. So with an army of ten thousand men on foot and in chariots, Thutmose III quelled the rebellion and held siege the city of Megiddo. It was the first known battle with precisely detailed events.

The whole Near Eastern campaign was a masterpiece of planning and nerve. It took him ten days to reach Gaza, he took the city and marched for Megiddo which was held by the rebellious prince of Kadesh. He led the campaign at the head of his army and routed the enemy who quickly scattered and fled in panic for safety within the walls of Megiddo. Unfortunately the Egyptian troops stopped their pursuit for loot and allowed their enemy to get away. Thutmose was forced to besiege the city instead, but he finally succeeded in conquering it after a siege of seven or eight months.

This campaign drastically changed the political situation in the ancient Near East. By taking Megiddo, Thutmose gained control of all of northern Canaan, and the Syrian princes were obligated to send tribute and their own sons as hostages to Egypt.

Death and burial: When Thutmose III died, his Great Royal Wife, Merytra Hatshepsut, survived him into the reign of their son as Queen Mother. Thutmose III was interred in the Valley of the Kings in tomb KV34. His mummy was found in the royal cache at Deir el Bahri.

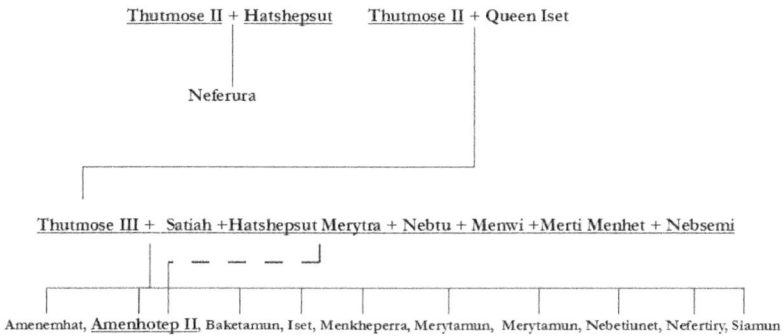

Thutmose II + Hatshepsut   Thutmose II + Queen Iset

Neferura

Thutmose III + Satiah +Hatshepsut Merytra + Nebtu + Menwi +Merti Menhet + Nebsemi

Amenemhat, Amenhotep II, Baketamun, Iset, Menkheperra, Merytamun, Merytamun, Nebetiunet, Nefertiry, Siamun

The Nine Bows

The Enemies of Ancient Egypt

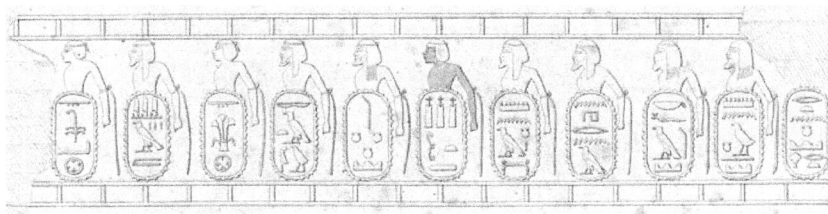

The nine bows was a term used by the ancient Egyptians to represent the enemies of Egypt. The Nine Bows list covered by this term changed over time, as enemies changed. When depicted the nine bows were usually shown as dressed differently from each other, as they each personify a specific enemy relevant to the time period:

 tA-Sma **Ta Shema** 'The Southern Enemies'

 sxtyw-gs **Sekhetyu-Ges** 'Peasant Border Enemies'

 ta-mHw **Ta Mehu** 'Northern Enemies'

 pDt-imntyw **Pedjet-Imentyu** 'Western Enemies'

THnw **Tjhenu** 'Libyans'

iwnwt-tA **Iunut-Ta** 'Nubian Enemies'

mn-tyw-nw-sTt **Imentyw-Setjet** 'Bedouins, Asiatics'

nhrn **Naharin**

kftyw **Keftyw** (Crete?) xftyw (enemy)

mntyw-st? **Mentyw Set** 'Nomads of Asia'

rtnw **Retjenu** (Lebanon, Syria)

kS **Kush** 'Upper Nubia'

irm **Irem** 'Sudan'

Queen Satiah

SAT-IAH

sAt-iah

daughter-moon

Sat-Iah

'Daughter of the Moon'

Spouse: Thutmose III

Children: possibly Prince Amenemhat

Father: possibly Ahmose Pen-Nekhebet, an important official, tutor to Neferura.

Mother: Ipu, a royal nurse

Died: Thebes?

Burial: Thebes?

Life: Satiah was the 'Great Royal Wife' of Thutmose III; she was the daughter of an important official, Ahmose Pen-Nekhebet, who also served as tutor to Hatshepsut's daughter, Neferura. It is possible that Prince Amenemhat, the elder son of Thutmose III, was her son. Amenemhat died before his father and so did not succeed the throne. Satiah died during her husband's reign; therefore Thutmose's next Great Royal Wife was Merytra-Hatshepsut. Satiah's titles include: 'King's Wife, Great King's Wife and God's Wife.'

An inscription showing the great royal wife Satiah
between two images of Thutmosis III.

Satiah is depicted as the same size as her husband and carries a sacred wand in her left hand and in her right hand a mace and ankh. She wears the Mut (Mother) headdress and uraeus. Her cartouche and titles read:

nsw-Hmt wr (sAt-iaH) anx-ti

king wife great (daughter-moon) live-she

Nesw-Hemet (Sat-Iah) Ankh-ti

'King's Great Wife, Daughter of the Moon, May She Live'

Thutmose III's cartouche and titles read:

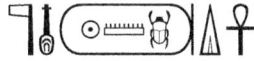

nfr-nTr (mn-xpr-ra) di anx

good-god (established-manifestation-Ra) given life

Nefer-Netjer (Men-kheper-Ra) di Ankh

'The Good God, Established are the Manifestation of Ra, given Life'

Merytra-Hatshepsut

MERYT-RA HAT-SHEPSUT

mryt-ra HAt-Spswt

beloved of Ra, foremost noble-lady

Meryt-Ra, Hat-shepsut

'Beloved of Ra, Foremost Noble Lady'

Husband: Pharaoh Thutmose III

Father: ?

Mother: Huy, a priestess of Amun and Atum during the 18t Dynasty

Children: Pharaoh Amenhotep II, Prince Menkheperra, Princess Nebetiunet, Princesses Merytamun C and D and Iset.

Burial: possibly KV42 or KV35

Life: Merytra-Hatshepsut is known to have held the titles: 'Hereditary Princess, Sole One, Great of Praises, King's Mother, Lady of The Two Lands, King's Wife, Great King's Wife, God's Wife and God's Hand.'

A scene from a tomb in Abd-el-Qurna shows Merytra with her son Amenhotep II with the titles:

nsw-mwt, nsw-Hmt wrt, Hmt-nTr, Drt-nTr

king's-mother, king's-wife great, god's-wife, god's-hand (beloved of Ra, foremost-lady) life she, Ra-like, forever

Nesw-Mut, Nesw-Hemet Weret, Hemet-Netjer, Djeret-Netjer (Meryt-Amun, Hat-sepsut) Ankh Ti, mi Ra, Djeta

'King's Mother, King's Great Wife, God's Wife, God's Hand (Beloved of Ra, Foremost Lady) She Lives, Like Ra, Forever'

Scene showing Merytra with her son Amenhotep II

Prince Amenemhat

m-HAt-imn

as/in the position of-foremost-Amun

Emhat-Amun

'The Foremost of Amun'

Father: Pharaoh Thutmose III

Mother: possibly Queen Satiah

Life: He was the eldest son and heir apparent of his father, pharaoh Thutmose III. It is possible that his mother was Queen Satiah. Prince Amenemhat was appointed to the position of 'Overseer of the Cattle,' an unusual title for a prince.

Amenemhat predeceased his father, so the next pharaoh was his half-brother Amenhotep II.

Princess Baketamun

bAkt-imn

maidservant-Amun

Baket-Amun

'Maidservant of Amun'

Father: Pharaoh Thutmose III

Mother: ?

Life: Baketamun was a princess of the Eighteenth dynasty of Egypt, a daughter of Pharaoh Thutmose III. Her name means 'Maidservant of Amun.'

Princess Iset

ist

Isis

Iset

Father: Pharaoh Thutmose III

Mother: Great Royal Wife Merytra-Hatshepsut

Life: Princess Iset (Isis) was a daughter of Pharaoh Thutmose III and his Great Royal Wife Merytra-Hatshepsut.

She was one of six known children of Thutmose and Merytra; her siblings are Pharaoh Amenhotep II, Prince Menkheperra and princesses Nebetiunet, Merytamun and the second Merytamun. She is depicted together with her sisters and Menkheperra on a statue of their maternal grandmother Huy (a priestess of Amun), she is depicted as smaller than her siblings and therefore is likely to have been the youngest of them.

Prince Menkheperra

⊙ ᴗᴗᴗᴗ 𓆣

mn-xpr-ra

established-manifestations-Ra

Men-khper-ra

'Enduring Manifestations of Ra'

Father: Pharaoh Thutmose III

Mother: Great Royal Wife Merytra Hatshepsut

Life: Menkheperra was a prince of the Eighteenth dynasty of Egypt, one of two known sons of Pharaoh Thutmose III and his Great Royal Wife Merytra-Hatshepsut. His name is the throne name of his father and means 'Enduring are the manifestations of Ra.'

He was one of six known children of Thutmose and Merytra Hatshepsut, his siblings are Pharaoh Amenhotep II, and princesses Nebetiunet, Merytamun, the second Merytamun and Iset. He is depicted together with his sisters on a statue of their maternal grandmother Huy, who was a priestess of Amun and the sun god Aten.

Princess Nebetiunet

nbt-iwnt

lady-pillar town (Denderah)

Nebet-Iunet

Lady of Iunet (Denderah)

Father: Pharaoh Thutmose III

Mother: Great Royal Wife Merytra Hatshepsut

Life: Princess Nebetiunet was a daughter of Pharaoh Thutmose III and his Great Royal Wife Merytra Hatshepsut. Her name means 'Lady of the Pillar Town (Denderah) which was a title of the goddess Hathor.

She is depicted together with her sisters and Menkheperra on a statue of their maternal grandmother, the priestess of Amun and the Aten, Huy.

Prince Siamun

SA-AMUN

sA-imn

son-Amun

Sa-Amun

'Son of Amun'

Father: Pharaoh Thutmose III

Mother: ?

Siblings: Amenemhat, Amenhotep II, Baketamun, Iset, Menkheperra, Merytamun, Merytamun, Nebetiunet, Nefertiry.

Life: Siamun (Sa-Amun) 'Son of Amun' was a prince of the eighteenth dynasty of Egypt, a son of Pharaoh Thutmose III.

▶

Family Tree of Amenhotep II

Thutmose III + Satiah + Hatshepsut Merytra + Nebtu + Menwi + Merti Menhet + Nebsemi

Amenemhat, Amenhotep II, Baketamun, Iset, Menkheperra, Merytamun, Merytamun, Nebetiunet, Nefertiry, Siamun

Amenhotep II + Queen Tia

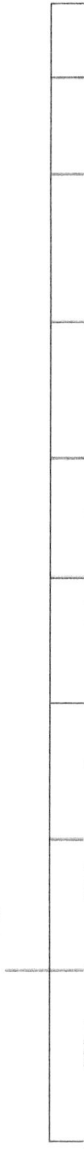

Tuthmose IV, Amenhotep, Webensenu, Amenemopet, Nedjem, Khaemwaset, Aaheperkara, Aakheperura, Iaret, Ahmose.

Amenhotep II - Aakheperura

HOTEP-AMUN

1427-1401 or 1427-1397 BC

Reign: 26 or 30 yrs

sA-ra (Htp-imn-HqA-iwnw)

son-Ra (satisfied-Amun-prince-Heliopolis)

Sa Ra (Hetep-Amun, Heqa Iunu)

'Son of Ra, Satisfied is Amun, Ruler of Heliopolis'

nswt bity (aA-xpr-w-ra)

king-south-north (great-manifestations-Ra)

Neswt Bity, Aa-kheper-u-Ra

'King of the South and North, Great the Manifestations of Ra'

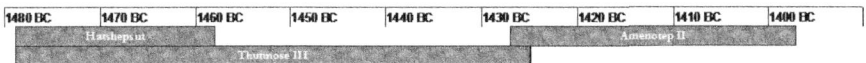

1480 BC	1470 BC	1460 BC	1450 BC	1440 BC	1430 BC	1420 BC	1410 BC	1400 BC
	Hatshepsut					Amenhotep II		
			Thutmose III					

Predecessor: Thutmose III

Successor: Thutmose IV

Consort: Queen Tiaa

Father: Thutmose III

Mother: Merytra Hatshepsut

Children: Pharaoh Thutmose IV, Amenhotep, Webensenu, Amenemopet, Nedjem, Khaemwaset, Aaheperkara, Aakheperura, Iaret, Ahmose.

Died: 1401 or 1397 BC

Burial: KV35

Reign: Amenhotep II was the seventh king of the 18th Dynasty and was born of Pharaoh Thutmose III and his minor wife, Merytra Hatshepsut. He was eighteen years old when he became king. Amenhotep II inherited a vast and prosperous kingdom from his father Thutmose III, and held it by means of a few military campaigns in Syria. He was an athletic youth and is depicted as being engaged in a number of sporting activities. He claims to have been able to shoot an arrow through a copper target one palm thick, and that he was able to row his ship faster and farther than two hundred members of the navy could row theirs.

At the death of his father, (and his elder brother Amenemhat), the Asiatic cities rose up in revolt; Amenhotep quickly showed them he was a king not to be toyed with. In the second year of his reign he led a military campaign and marched north into Palestine, he fought his way across the Orontes River in northern Syria and subdued all before him. He is said to have singlehandedly killed 7 rebel Princes at Kadesh, which successfully terminated his first Syrian campaign on a victorious note. After the campaign, the king ordered the bodies of the seven princes to be hung upside down on the prow of his ship. Upon reaching Thebes all but one of the princes were mounted on the city walls. The other was taken to the often rebellious territory of Nubia and hung on the city wall of Napata, as an example of the consequence of rebellion against the Pharaoh and to demoralise any Nubian opponents of Egyptian authority there.

Death and Burial: Amenhotep II was interred in KV35 in the Valley of the Kings, but his tomb was robbed by the end of the 20th Dynasty. Amenhotep's mummy was discovered in March 1898 by Victor Loret in his KV35 tomb in the Valley of the Kings within his original sarcophagus.

Queen Tiaa

TI-AA

Ⓝ 𝕀𝕀𝕄

ti-aA

she-great

Ti-aa

'The Great'

Consort: Pharaoh Amenhotep II

Children: Pharaoh Thutmose IV

Burial: Tomb KV32

Life: Queen Tiaa was the wife of Pharaoh Amenhotep II and mother of Thutmose IV. During the reign of her husband she was never called 'King's Daughter' and is of uncertain parentage. During her son's reign she received the title of 'Great Royal Wife, King's Mother and God's Wife.'

Titles: 'Hereditary Princess, Hereditary Princess in the Per-Wer (Great-House), Great of Grace, Great of Praises, Sweet of Love, She who sees Horus and Seth, King's Mother, King's Wife, Great King's Wife, Wife of the Dual King, God's Wife, God's Hand, Mistress of the Entire Two Lands, Attendant of Horus, Lady of all Women, Daughter of Geb.'

Burial: Tiaa was buried in KV32 in the Valley of the Kings

Prince Amenhotep

Htp-imn

satisfied-Amun

Hotep-Amun

'Amun is Satisfied'

Life: Amenhotep was an Ancient Egyptian prince during the 18th dynasty, son and (possibly) the designated heir of Amenhotep II.

He was a priest of Ptah and is mentioned in an administrative papyrus. A stela near the Great Sphinx, showing a priest of Ptah whose name was erased, probably depicts him. It is likely that he died young, for the next pharaoh was his brother Thutmose IV.

Prince Webensenu

Father: Amenhotep II

Mother: ?

Webensenu was an ancient Egyptian prince of the 18th dynasty. He was a son of Pharaoh Amenhotep II. He is mentioned, along with his brother Nedjem, on a statue of Minmose, overseer of the workmen in Karnak. There is evidence that he headed the chariotry

imy-r ssm.wt 'Overseer of the Horses (Chariotry)'

ssm.wt 'horses'

wrrt 'Chariot'

Prince Webensenu '...had access to is father, without being announced,' and that he '...body guarded the king of Upper and Lower Egypt.'

Death and Burial: He died as a child and was buried in his father's tomb, KV35. His mummy is still there. Tomb KV35, contained some objects of Prince Webensenu's burial, his mummy appears to be that of a young 11 year old boy wearing the platted side-lock of youth.

Prince Amunemopet

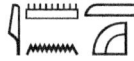

imn-m ipt

Amun in harem

Amun-em-ipet

Father: Amenhotep II?

Mother: ?

Life: Amunemopet was an Ancient Egyptian prince during the 18th dynasty, probably a son of Amenhotep II. He is known from the so-called Stela C found in the Sphinx temple of Amenhotep II. He is identified as a son of this pharaoh based on the stela, which is stylistically datable to the reign of Amenhotep II. It is possible that he is the Prince Amenemopet shown on the stela of the royal nurse Senetruiu.

Prince Nedjem

nDm

sweet

Nedjem

'Sweet (of flavour)'

Father: Amenhotep II

Mother: ?

Life: Prince Nedjem was a son of Pharaoh Amenhotep II.   He is known from only one source: he is mentioned, along with his brother Webensenu, on a statue of Minmose, overseer of the workmen in Karnak

Prince Kaemwaset

xA-m-wAst

appearing-in-Thebes

Ka-em-waset

'Appearing in Thebes.'

Father: Amenhotep II

Mother: ?

Life: Prince Kaemwaset is likely to have been a son of Pharaoh Amenhotep II. He is mentioned on two graffiti along with the throne name of Amenhotep II. He is titled 'Overseer of the Cattle,' which was a rare title for a prince.

Princess Iaret

iart

uraeus

Iaret

Consort: Thutmose IV (brother and husband)

Father: Amenhotep II

Children: unknown

Life: Married her brother and became his Great Royal Wife (see Queen Iaret).

Family Tree: Thutmose IV

Amenhotep II + Queen Tia

Tuthmose IV, Amenhotep, Webensenu, Amenemopet, Nedjem, Khaemwaset, Aaheperkara, Aakheperura, Iaret, Ahmose.

Thutmose IV + Nefertari + Iaret + Mutemwiya

Amenhotep III, Siatum, Amenemhat, Tiaa, Amenemopet, Petepihu, Tentamun

Princess Nebtia

MOSE-DJHUTY

MEN-KHEPER-U-RA

1401-1391 or 1397-1388 BC

Reign 10 or 9 yrs

sA ra (DHwty-ms)

son Ra (Mose-Djhuty)

Sa Ra, Mose-Djhuty

'Son of Ra, Born of Djhuty'

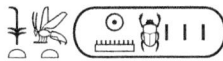

nswt bity (mn-xpr-w-ra)

king-south king-north (established-manifestations-Ra)

Neswt Bity (Men-kheper-Ra)

'King of the South and North,

Enduring are the Manifestations of Ra'

123

Predecessor: Pharaoh Amenhotep II

Successor: Pharaoh Amenhotep III

Consort: Nefertari, Iaret, Mutemwiya

Father: Pharaoh Amenhotep II

Mother: Queen Tiaa

Children: Pharaoh Amenhotep III, Siatum, Amenemhat, Tiaa, Amenemopet, Petepihu, Tentamun

Died: 1391 or 1388 BC

Burial: KV43

Reign: Thutmose IV was the 8th king of the 18th Dynasty; he was born of Amenhotep II and Queen Tia.

Thutmose IV was not the heir apparent (Crown Prince) to the throne; this title probably belonged to his brother Amenhotep, a Priest of Ptah, who died young. Thutmose IV justified his claim to the throne by the erection and declaration of the Dream Stela which was placed between the paws of the Great Sphinx:

The Dream Stela

While the young prince Thutmose was out on a hunting trip, he stopped to rest under the head of the Sphinx, which at that time was buried up to the neck in sand. He soon fell asleep and had a dream in which the Sphinx told him that if he cleared away the sand and restored it he would become the next Pharaoh. After completing the restoration of the Sphinx, he placed a carved stone tablet, now known as the Dream Stela, between the two paws of the Sphinx. The

124

restoration of the Sphinx and the text of the Dream Stele was probably a piece of propaganda meant to bestow legitimacy upon his unexpected kingship.

The winged sun disc (laced with a pair of cobras) spread out over the whole inscription is a representation of Ra-Horakhety, a combination of the sun god Ra and Horus of the Two Horizons (Ra, who is Horus of the Two Horizons).

The whole inscription is a symmetrical presentation of Thutmose IV making offerings to the Great Sphinx, **Hor-em-Akhet** 'Horus in the Horizon' which represents the sun in its early rising:

 Hr-m-Axt '**Hor-em-Akhet**, Horus in the Horizon'

Hor-em-akhet: was often depicted as a sphinx with the head of a man, a lion or a ram. It is often suggested that the Great Sphinx of Giza is a representation of Hor-em-akhet with the face of the fourth dynasty pharaoh Kafra (Chephren). He was also depicted as a falcon or as a man with the head of a falcon wearing a variety of crowns.

Either side of a column of Thutmose IV's titles is an image of the recumbent Horus-in-the-Horizon upon a shrine. On the left

Thutmose IV offers a jar of wine or water to the Sphinx and on the right he is depicted as offering a water libation and incense.

Military Campaigns

Little is known about his brief ten-year rule. He suppressed a minor uprising in Nubia in his 8th year around 1393 BC and was referred to in a stela as the Conqueror of Syria. Thutmose IV's rule is significant because he was the New Kingdom pharaoh who established peaceful relations with Mitanni and married a Mitannian princess to seal this new alliance. One of the Amarna Letters written after Thutmose IV's reign by Tushratta, the King of Mitanni to Amenhotep IV (Akhenaten) states:

'When [Menkheperra], the father of Nimmureya (Amenhotep III) wrote to Artatama, my grandfather, he asked for the daughter of my grandfather, the sister of my father. He wrote 5, 6 times, but he did not give her. When he wrote my grandfather 7 times, then only under such pressure, did he give her.'

Like most of the kings of the early half of the 18th Dynasty, Thutmose IV built on a grand scale. He completed an obelisk first started by Thutmose III, which, at 32 m (105 ft), was the tallest obelisk ever erected in Egypt, at the Temple of Karnak. Thutmose IV called it the **Tekhen Waty** or 'Unique Obelisk.'

Death and Burial

Thutmose IV died after about ten years of reign and was buried in Tomb KV43 in the Valley of the Kings. His tomb was robbed shortly after and its later restoration was recorded during the reign of Horemheb. The officials Maya and Djhutymose were responsible for its restoration. Thutmose IV's mummy was found in a cache of mummies in KV35, the tomb of Amenhotep II.

Queen Nefertari

NEFERT-IRY

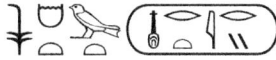

nsw Hmt wrt (nfrt-iry)

king wife great (beautiful-lady)

News Hemet Weret (Neferet-iry)

'King's Great Wife, Beautiful Lady'

Spouse: Pharaoh Thutmose IV

Father: ?

Mother: ?

Children: ?

Life: Nefertari was the Great Royal Wife of Thutmose IV, little is known about her and she may have been a commoner.

On several depictions she and Queen Mother Tiaa are depicted as goddesses accompanying Thutmose. In the 7th year the new Great Royal Wife was Thutmose's sister Iaret, Nefertari either died or was pushed into the background when Iaret was old enough to become Thutmose's wife.

Queen Iaret

iart

uraeus

Iaret

'Uraeus'

Consort: Thutmose IV (brother and husband)

Father: Amenhotep II

Children: unknown

Life: Queen Iaret was the daughter of Amenhotep II and wife and sister of Thutmose IV. The transcription of her name is uncertain, it is written with a single cobra, which has a number of possible readings.

The uraeus **iart**, was used as a symbol of sovereignty, royalty, deity, and divine authority in ancient Egypt. The Uraeus is a symbol for the goddess Wadjet, who was one of the earliest Egyptian deities and who was often depicted as a cobra. The centre of her cult was in Per-Wadjet (House of Wadjet), later called Buto by the Greeks.

Her titles include: 'King's Daughter, Great King's Daughter, King's Sister and King's Great Wife.' In an inscription she is depicted standing behind her husband Thutmose IV who is portrayed by convention slaying his enemy:

The stela depicts Tuthmosis smiting enemies before the Nubian gods Dedwen and Ha.

Queen Iaret is depicted standing behind him.

The titles above her head read:

nsw sAt, nsw Snt (Iart) nsw Hmt wrt

king daughter, king sister (Uraeus) king wife great

Nesw Sat, Nesw Senet (Iaret) Nesw Hemet Weret

'The King's Daughter, The King's Sister (Uraeus) The King's Great Wife'

There are no known children for Queen Iaret and it is not known when she died or where she was buried.

Queen Mutemwiya

MUT-EM-WIA

mwt-m-wiA

mother-in-sacred bark

Mut-em-wia

'Mother Goddess Mut in the Sacred Bark of the River'

Spouse: Pharaoh Thutmose IV

Children: Pharaoh Amenhotep III

Life: Mutemwiya was a minor wife of Thutmose IV and the mother of Pharaoh Amenhotep III. Mutemwiya's name means 'Mut in the divine bark.'

At the court of Thutmose IV were two other Queens, before her was Queen Nefertari and later Queen Iaret. Most of what is known about her comes from the monuments of her son, Amenhotep III. She may have been the daughter of the Mitannian king, Artatama I.

Mutemwiya held many titles including 'God's Wife, Lady of The Two Lands, Great King's Wife, His Beloved, Noblewoman, Countess, Great of Praises, Sweet of Love, Mistress of Upper and Lower Egypt, and God's Mother.' The titles king's mother and god's mother amount to the same thing since the god in question was the reigning king, Amenhotep III. All of these titles, including that of Great Royal Wife, were used only after her husband's death, during her son's reign. At the time of Amenhotep III's accession to the throne she gained prominence as the new pharaoh's mother.

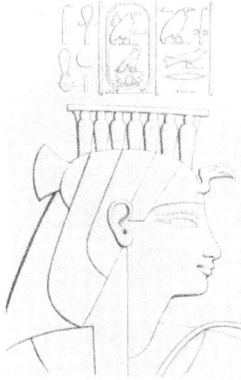

Queen Mutemwiya of the 18th dynasty of Ancient Egypt.

Mother of Amenhotep III. From Luxor

The inscription gives her title:

nsw mwt wrt (mwt-em-wia) anx ti ra mi

king mother great (Mut-in-sacred boat) live she Ra like

Nesw Mut Weret (Mut-em-wia) Ankh ti, Ra mi

'King's Great Mother, Mut in her Sacred Bark, She Lives, Like Ra'

Mutemwiya is shown in the Luxor temple, in scenes depicting the divine birth of her son Amenhotep III. The scenes show Amenhotep III to be the result of the union of his mother with the god Amun himself (portrayed in the form of her husband, Thutmose IV).

Death and Burial: unknown

131

Prince Siatum

SA-ITEMU

sA-itmw

son-Atu

Sa-Itumw

'Son of Atum'

Spouse: ?

Father: Pharaoh Thutmose IV

Mother: ?

Children: a daughter named Princess Nebetia.

Siblings: Pharaoh Amenhotep III, Amenemhat, Tiaa, Amenemopet, Petepihu, Tentamun

Life: Prince Siatum was likely to be one of the sons of Pharaoh Thutmose IV and thus the brother or half-brother of Amenhotep III.

A mummy label was found on the mummy of his daughter in the Sheikh Abd el-Qurna cache, which mentions Prince Siatum as her father. It is possible that his tutor was named Meryra from a statue dated to the reign of Amenhotep III. The statue shows a person named Siatum sat on Meryra's lap.

Princess Nebetia

NEBET-IA

nbt-iA

lady-praise and adoration

Nebet-ia

'Adored Lady'

Grandfather: Pharaoh Thutmose IV

Father: Prince Siatum

Titles: 'King's Daughter'

Buried: mummy found in the Sheikh Abd el-Qurna cache.

Life: there is little evidence about her life except the fact that she was the daughter of Prince Siatum and that she had the title of 'King's Daughter' which is unusual considering that Siatum did not become Pharaoh.

▶

Family Tree: Amenhotep III

Artatama I

Shuttarna II

Atashumara

Thutmose IV + Nefertari + Iaret + Mutemwiya

Amenhotep III, Siatum, Amenemhat, Tiaa, Amenemopet, Petepihu, Tentamun

Princess Nebtia

Tushratta + Juni

Yuya + Tuya

Tiye + Amenhotep III + Gilukhepa + Tadukhepa + Nebetnehat + Satamun (yr 30)

Ay, Anen

Akhenaten, Prince Tuthmose, Satamun, Iset, Henuttaneb, Nebetah, Smenkkara? Baketaten, Nebetnehat?

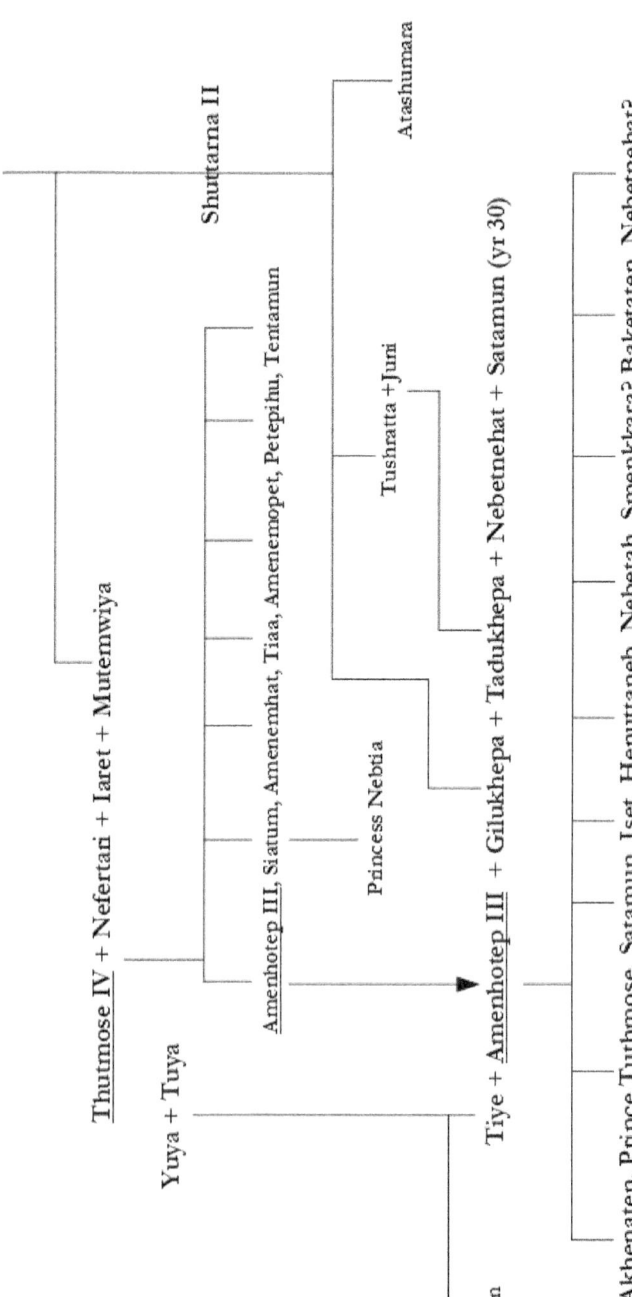

HOTEP-AMUN

1391-1353 or 1388-1351 BC

Reign: 37 - 38 yrs

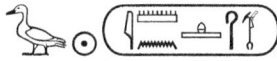

sA ra (Htp-Imn, HqA wAst

son Ra (satisfied-Amun, ruler Thebes)

Sa Ra, Hotep-Amun, Heqa Waset

'Son of Ra, Satisfied is Amun, Ruler of Thebes'

nswt bity (nb-mAat-ra)

king-south-north (lord-truth-Ra)

Neswt Bity, Neb-Maat-Ra

'King of Egypt, Lord of Truth is Ra'

1400 BC	1390 BC	1380 BC	1370 BC	1360 BC	1350 BC	1340 BC
Thutmose IV		Amenhotep III			Amenhotep IV - Akhenaten	

Predecessor: Thutmose IV

Successor: Akhenaten

Consorts: Tiye, Gilukhepa, Tadukhepa, Nebetnehat, Satamun (yr 30)

Father: Pharaoh Thutmose IV

Mother: Queen Mutemwiya

Children: Akhenaten, Prince Thutmose, Satamun, Iset, Henuttaneb, Nebetah, Smenkkara? Baketaten, Nebetnehat?

Died: 1353 or 1352 BC

Burial: Western arm of the Valley of the Kings WV22

Reign: Amenhotep III was the 9th pharaoh of the 18th Dynasty. The son of Thutmose IV and a minor wife Mutemwiya and the father of the Amenhotep IV (Akhenaten), Amenhotep III was born around 1388 BC. His reign was a period of unprecedented prosperity and artistic splendour, when Egypt reached the peak of its artistic and international power. When he died in the 38th or 39th year of his reign, his son initially ruled as Amenhotep IV, but then changed his own royal name to Akhenaten. His great-grandfather Thutmose III, had laid down the splendour and wealth of the Egyptian empire of the 18th Dynasty by his campaigns into Syria, Nubia and Libya. Under the reign of Amenhotep III there were few military campaigns and those that did occur were directed by his son, Merymose, Viceroy of Kush.

It is possible that is mother, Queen Mutemwiya, was the daughter of the Mitannian king, Artatama. Amenhotep III had a large and ever increasing harem, several of which were foreign princesses. His chief wife Tiye was of non-royal birth. She was the daughter of a noble called Yuya and his wife Tuya. Yuya was an important noble owning land in the north Delta region and he was a powerful military leader.

Tiye's brother Anen rose to power during this period and became 'Chancellor of the King of Lower Egypt,' he also had the titles of 'Second Prophet of Amun, Sem Priest of Heliopolis' and 'Divine Father.' Tiye's other brother, Ay, assumed the throne after the death of Tutankhamun.

Tiye gave birth to at least six children, at least two sons and four daughters. The eldest son, Prince Thutmose, died without reigning; leaving his younger brother Amenhotep IV (Akhenaten) heir to the throne.

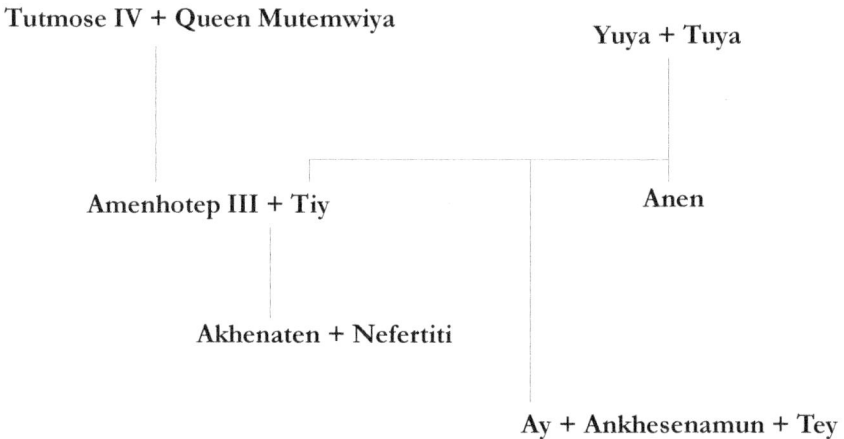

Tutmose IV + Queen Mutemwiya

Yuya + Tuya

Amenhotep III + Tiy

Anen

Akhenaten + Nefertiti

Ay + Ankhesenamun + Tey

Amenhotep III married two of his daughters, first Iset and then in year 30 of his reign, Princess Satamun, his eldest daughter, both were given the title of 'Great Royal Wife.' Amenhotep III has the most surviving statues of any Egyptian pharaoh. Over 200 large commemorative stone scarabs have been discovered from his reign over a large geographic area ranging from Syria through to Soleb in Nubia. Five large scarabs document the first 12 years of his reign:

Year 2: The Marriage Scarab: records Amenhotep's marriage to Queen Tiye.

Year 2: Sporting Scarab: this scarab records his sporting prowess and how he captured 556 wild cattle in a single day.

Lion Hunt Scarab: records that he slew 102 fierce lions in the first ten years of his reign.

Arrival of Princess Gilukhepa Scarab: this scarab documents the arrival of Princess Gilukhepa, daughter of King Shuttarna II of Mitanni, to join Amenhotep's harem. (see Appendix #28)

Year 11: Digging of a Pleasure Lake: this scarab documents that Amenhotep III has a pleasure lake dug for Queen Tiye to sail upon. The lake was huge, it was over a mile long and about a quarter of a mile wide. The king and queen celebrated its opening by sailing over it in the royal barge named the 'Aten Gleams.'

The Arrival Scarab of Princess Gilukhipa (Kyrgypa):

'Regnal Year 10 under the Majesty of the Horus...'

This is followed by the full titles of Amenhotep III:

'Strong Bull appearing in Truth, He of the Two Goddesses, Establishing Laws, Pacifying the Two Lands, Golden Horus, Great of Valour, Smiting the Asiatics, King of Upper and Lower Egypt, Neb-Maat-Ra, Son of Ra, Amenhotep, Ruler of Thebes, given Life, ...:'

'King's Great Wife (Ty) may she Live.'

'The name of her father, Yuia, the name of her mother, Tjuia.'

'Marvel brought to his Majesty, Life, Prosperity and Health.'

'The daughter-elder, of the Prince of Naharina (Nhrna),

Shutarna (Sa-ti-r-na)'

'Gilukhiper (Kyr-gy-pa), chief women of her harem, three hundred
and seventeen women.'

Amenhotep III's lengthy reign was a period of unprecedented
prosperity and artistic splendour, when Egypt reached the peak of its
artistic and international power. Proof of this is shown by the
diplomatic correspondence from the rulers of Assyria, Mitanni,
Babylon, and Hatti which are preserved in the archive of Amarna
Letters; these letters document frequent requests by these rulers for
gold and numerous other gifts from the pharaoh.

Amenhotep III celebrated three Jubilee Sed festivals, in his Year 30,
Year 34, and Year 37 respectively at his Malkata summer palace in
Western Thebes. The palace was called Per-Hay or 'House of
Rejoicing.'

He undertook many building works at Karnak and Luxor; his statues
include the two giant 60 ft high seated statues of himself known as the

Colossi of Memnon on the West Bank near his later demolished mortuary temple.

Amenhotep III's Co-regency with Akhenaten

There has been much debate over the years as to a possible co-regency between Amenhotep III and his son Akhenaten, some evidence suggests that this lasted for a possible two or twelve years. At Amarna, the city of Akhenaten and his father, the two royal families are shown together and it seems likely that they co-ruled Egypt for some considerable amount of time, this long-co-regency has been re-enforced by some new discoveries: The Egyptian Ministry for Antiquities announced what it called conclusive evidence that Akhenaten shared power with his father for at least 8 years, based on the evidence coming from the tomb of Vizier Amenhotep-Huy.

The inscriptions were carved onto architectural remains, collapsed walls and columns, in tomb number 28 in the El Asasif area of Luxor. Some of the inscriptions depict scenes of father and son together in the same space as one follows the other. There are also cartouches, the pre-nomen or throne name of a pharaoh surrounded by a protective oval, of both pharaohs next to each other. Traditionally, viziers' tombs always bear the cartouche of the pharaoh they served under.

Death and Burial: Amenhotep III died in year 39 of his reign when he was about 45 years old, he was interred in WV22. Sometime during the Third Intermediate Period his mummy was moved from this tomb and was placed in a side-chamber of KV35 along with several other pharaohs of the Eighteenth and Nineteenth dynasties where it lay until discovered by Victor Loret in 1898.

Queen Tiye

TIY

Royal Court: 1390 - 1353 BC   37 yrs

Lived: 49 yrs

𓏏𓍯𓇓𓐠𓇌𓏏𓆑𓏏𓇋

nsw Hmt wrt (Tiy) anx ti

king wife great (Tiy) live she

Nesw Hemet Weret (Tiy) Ankh Ti

'Kings' Great Wife, Tiy, may She Live'

Spouse: Pharaoh Amenhotep III

Father: Yuya

Mother: Tuya

Children: Satamun, Great Royal Wife Iset, Great Royal Wife Princess, Henuttaneb, Princess Nebetah, Crown Prince Thutmose, Akhenaten, Smenkhkara? The Younger Lady, Princess Baketaten.

Born: 1398 BC

Died: 1338 BC

Life: Queen Tiye was the daughter of Yuia and Tjuia. She became the Great Royal Wife of Pharaoh Amenhotep III and gave him many children, including the next Pharaoh, Amenhotep IV (Akhenaten). She was the grandmother of Tutankhamun and possibly the mother of his elder brother Pharaoh Smenkhkara.

Tiye's father, Yuia, was a non-royal, but a wealthy landowner from the Upper Egyptian town of Akhmin, where he served as a priest and superintendent of oxen or commander of the chariotry. Tiye's mother, Tjuia, was involved in many religious cults, her title included 'Singer of Hathor,' and 'Chief of the Entertainers of Amun and Min.' Tiye's brother Anen was the Second Prophet (Priest) of Amun, it is also speculated that the Pharaoh Ay was also her brother. Because of her long life and position of power she exerted great influence in the royal court during the time of her husband Amenhotep III and her son's reigns.

Tiye is known to have outlived Amenhotep III for as many as twelve years. She continued to be mentioned in the Amarna letters and in inscriptions as queen and beloved of the king. An Amarna letter which was addressed to Tiye dates to the reign of Akhenaten. She is known to have had a house at Amarna, Akhenaten's new capital.

Death and Burial: Tiye married Amenhotep III at the age of twelve, was at the royal court for 37 years and died at the age of 49 yrs, probably during the 12th year of Akhenaten's reign. There is the possibility of a long 12 year co-regency between Amenhotep III and Akhenaten (Year 1-12)

Tiye is believed to have been buried in Akhenaten's Tomb at Amarna, but her gilded burial shrine ended up in Tomb KV55. Her mummified remains was found adjacent to two other mummies in an opposite side chamber of Amenhotep II in KV35.

Tadukhipa

Consort: Amenhotep III, Amenhotep IV (Akhenaten)

Father: King Tushratta of Mitanni

Mother: Queen Juni

Life: Tadukhipa was the daughter of Tushratta, king of Mitanni and his queen Juni, and niece of Artashumara. Tadukhipa's aunt Gilukhipa (sister of Tushratta) had married Pharaoh Amenhotep III in his 10th regnal year. Tadukhipa was to marry Amenhotep III more than two decades later:

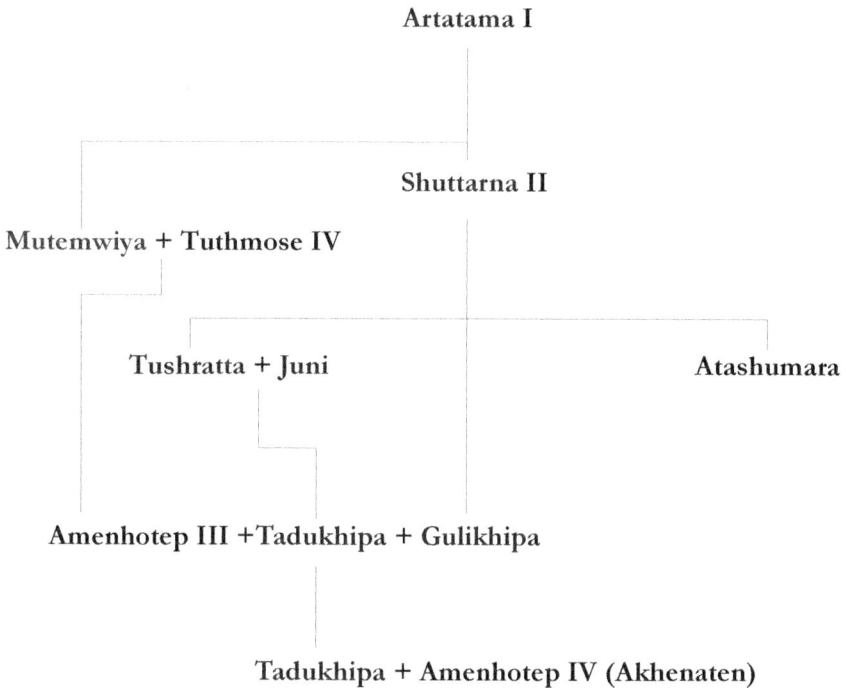

Artatama I

Shuttarna II

Mutemwiya + Tuthmose IV

Tushratta + Juni   **Atashumara**

Amenhotep III +Tadukhipa + Gulikhipa

Tadukhipa + Amenhotep IV (Akhenaten)

From the family tree the influence of Mitannian blood on the genealogy of the Dynasty can be clearly seen. Thutmose IV married Mutemwiya who is thought to be the daughter of the Mitannian king, Artatama I. Shuttarna's daughter, Gilukhipa, married Amenhotep III and later married Tadukhipa, also a Mitannian Princess and daughter of Tushratta. Then Amenhotep III's son Akhenaten also took Tadukhipa as his wife. This marriage of Egypt's Pharaoh's to daughters of the King's of Mitanni obviously cemented relationships between the two kingdoms.

Princess & Queen

Satamun

SAT-AMUN

sAt-imn

daughter-Amun

Sat-Amun

'Daughter of Amun'

Consort: Pharaoh Amenhotep III

Father: probably Amenhotep III (Year 30 of is reign), Thutmose IV an unproven probability.

Mother: probably Queen Tiye

Siblings: Prince Thutmose, Amenhotep IV (Akhenaten), Iset, Henuttaneb, Nebetah, Smenkhkare? Baketaten Nebetnehat?

Birth: 1370 BC - unknown

Burial: unknown, WV22 Amenhotep's tomb was intended for her.

Life: Satamun was the eldest daughter of Amenhotep III and his Great Royal Wife, Queen Tiye. Satamun married Amenhotep III around year 30 of his reign (the first Jubilee Year).

A chair of Satamun's was found in the tombs of Yuia and Tjuia (Tiye's parents) which bears her title of 'King's Daughter', thus stating she was the daughter of a Pharaoh and suggesting that she was a daughter of Amenhotep III and Tiye:

nsw sAt wr, mrt.f

king daughter great, beloved.his

'King's Great Daughter, His beloved.'

In fact there were three chairs of different sizes belonging to Satamun found in the tomb, suggesting they had been used by her as she grew up.

A blue faience eye paint (kohl) tube exists which bears her titles and connection with Amenhotep III (Neb-Maat-Ra) as her father and consort:

nfr-nTr (nb-mAat-ra) nsw sAt, nsw Hmt wrt (sAt-imn) anx ti

'Good god Neb-Maat-Ra, King's Daughter, King's Great Wife, Sat-Amun, She Lives.'

Titles of Satamun:

'Singer of the Lord of the Two Lands, King's Wife, King's Great Wife, King's Daughter, King's Daughter Whom He Loves, Eldest Daughter of the King and Great Daughter of the King Whom He Loves.'

In the last decade of her father's reign, she was promoted to the status of Great Royal Wife. The evidence for this marriage consists of a blue-faience kohl-tube with the cartouches of Amenhotep III and Satamun, an alabaster bowl found at Amarna with the same cartouches and jar-label inscriptions from Malkata palace. Satamun's elevation to her role as Great Royal Wife of her father, Amenhotep III, is attested as early as Year 30 of his reign from jar label inscription No.95 which was discovered in the royal palace. She maintained her own rooms in the Malkata palace complex, and Amenhotep, son of Hapu was appointed as the steward of her properties there. Although Satamun, as eldest daughter of the king was an important woman, she vanishes from the records at the end of Amenhotep III's reign and is not mentioned during Akhenaten's reign.

Death and Burial: A separate chamber was carved for her in Amenhotep III's tomb (WV22) in the Valley of the Kings, but there is no evidence that she was ever buried there. Her mummy has not been found.

Princess & Queen Iset

ISET

ist

'Iset'

Father: Pharaoh Amenhotep III

Mother: Queen Tiye GRW

Life: Princess Iset was a daughter of Amenhotep III and his Great Royal Wife Tiye; she was a sister of Crown Prince Thutmose and Akhenaten. Satamun was her elder sister.

Princess Iset married her father during the second Jubilee in year 34 of his reign.

Death and burial: after the death of her father she disappears from records.

Princess Henuttaneb

HENUT-TA-NEB

Hnwt-tA-nb

mistress-land-lord

Henut-ta-neb

'Mistress of the Lord of the Land'

Father: Amenhotep III

Mother: Queen Tiye

Siblings: Prince Thutmose, Satamun, Akhenaten, Iset, Nebetah, Smenkhkare? Baketaten, Nebetnehat.

Life: Henuttaneb was a daughter of Amenhotep III and his GRW Queen Tiye. She was a sister of Akhenaten.

She appears on a giant statue of the seated Amenhotep III and his wife Tiye, along with her two sisters, Nebetah and an unknown princess.

Henuttaneb's statue stands taller than the other two. It is not known if she married her father, but her name was found enclosed in a cartouche, the privilege of kings and queens. After the death of Amenhotep III she disappears from records.

Princess Nebetah

NEBET-AH

nbt-aH

lady-palace

Nebet-ah

'Lady of the Palace'

Father: Amenhotep III

Mother: Queen Tiye

Siblings: Prince Thutmose, Satamun, Akhenaten, Iset, Henuttaneb, Smenkhkare? Baketaten, Nebetnehat.

Life: Nebet-ah was a daughter of Pharaoh Amenhotep III and his GRW Queen Tiye; she was probably the youngest of her siblings and was depicted with her sister Henuttaneb in a giant statue of the seated Amenhotep III and Tiye.

There is no evidence that she married Amenhotep III, her only known title is 'King's Daughter Whom He loves.' After her father's death she disappears from record.

Beketaten

BAKET-ITEN

bAkt-itn

maidservant-Iten

Baket-Iten

'Maidservant of the Aten'

Father: Amenhotep III

Mother: Queen Tiye

Siblings: Prince Thutmose, Satamun, Akhenaten, Iset, Henuttaneb, Nebetah, Smenkhkare? Nebetnehat.

Life: Baketaten was probably the youngest daughter of Amenhotep II and his GRW Queen Tiye; she only appears after the Atenist reforms of Akhenaten, whereas Nebetah only appears before the reforms, and therefore, Baketaten and Nebetah may be one and the same person. During these reforms Amenhotep IV changed his name to Akhenaten and similarly Nebetah may have changed her name to Baketaten, although there is now proof that they are the same person.

Princess & Queen

Nebetnehat

NEBET-NEHET

⏝ 〰 ⌂ 🌳

lady-sycamore

Nebet-nehet

'Lady of the Sycamore'

Father: Amenhotep III?

Mother: Queen Tiye?

Siblings: Prince Thutmose, Satamun, Akhenaten, Iset, Henuttaneb, Smenkhkare? Baketaten

Life: Nebetnehat was a queen and Great Royal Wife of the 18th Dynasty to an unidentified Pharaoh. She may have been the mother of Ankhesenpaaten Tasherit and Meritaten Tasherit. Her name was found on an alabaster canopic fragment from the valley of the Queens. The inscription on the jar fragment reads:

nsw Hmt wr, mrt.f (nbt-nht)

king wife great, beloved.his (nbt-nht)

Nesw Hemet Weret, Meret.ef (Nebet-Nehet)

'King's Great Wife, His Beloved, Lady of the Sycamore'

Her name 'Lady of the Sycamore' is a reference to the goddess Hathor. The sycamore tree has long held a relationship with the goddess Hathor in the religious practices of ancient Egypt. The Hathoric sycamore cults appear to have originated in the Memphite area. Three main titles, and it also seems, three main cults, emerged referencing the goddess and the sycamore. These include: 'Mistress of the Sycamore, Mistress of the Sycamore in all her Places, and Mistress of the Southern Sycamore.'

Crown Prince Thutmose

MOSE-DJHUTY

𓇋𓏏𓀀

Father: Amenhotep III

Mother: possibly Queen Tiye.

Siblings: Satamun, Akhenaten, Iset, Henuttaneb, Nebetah, Smenkhkare? Baketaten, Nebetnehat.

Life: Prince Thutmose was Crown Prince of Egypt (Elder son and heir to the throne) under the reign of his father Pharaoh Amenhotep III. The name Mose-Djhuty means 'Born of the God Djhuty.

Prince Thutmose was given the titles 'Eldest King's Son, High Priest of Ptah at Memphis, Sem-Priest of Ptah at Memphis, Overseer of the Prophets of Upper and Lower Egypt.' This prince never inherited the throne, neither was he buried in the Valley of the Kings with other members of the royal family, he simply disappears from record between years 27 and 33 of his father's reign, his untimely disappearance led to the younger son Akhenaten taking the throne.

He may also have had connections to the military as an ivory whip found in the tomb of the boy king Tutankhamun is inscribed with the titles 'The King's son, the troop commander, Thutmose, repeating of births.'

Prince Thutmose' Cat (Ta-Miw)

The funeral item mentioning the prince as priest is the sarcophagus of a cat, presumably his pet named Ta Miw (The Cat); it was allegedly found at Mit Rahina, which suits the location of Djhutmose's official activity. It gives his fullest known titulary:

'sa (son)-nsw (king) smsw (eldest), imy-r (overseer) hmw-ntr (priest) m (in) Smaw (South) tA-mhw (Land-North), wr xrp hmw (Great Controller Priests, sm (Sem Priest)'

'Crown Prince, Overseer of the Priests of Upper and Lower Egypt, High Priest of Ptah in Memphis and Sem-Priest.'

The Bier Statuette

Prince Thutmose is depicted as being deceased and laying on a bier with a Ba (soul) bird on his chest. The inscription mentions 'the King's Son, Sem Priest, Thutmose.' .

The inscribed text:

HD nsw sA, sm Dhwty-ms, maA-xrw

destroyed/damage king son, Sem Priest Djhuty-mose, True Voice

'Destroyed the King's son, the Sem Priest Thutmose justified.'

Note the use of the word ⌐⌐x HD:

⌐⌐x HD 'to injure, destroy, annihilate, put an end to, with **ib** to disobey the heart'

Gardiner has this as: ⌐⌐x HDi 'be destroyed, perished, be lacking, fail, injure, disobey, annul, eclipse, degrade, destruction.'

155

The prince seems to have died during the third decade of the reign of Amenhotep III.

Apis Bull Inscription

He is also shown assisting Amenhotep III in administrative and religious capacities (such as a burial of an Apis bull).   When Apis Chapel I was uncovered by Mariette, it shows Amenhotep III accompanied by his son Prince Thutmose making the offering of incense to the bull of Memphis:

nsw sA, sm ms-DHwty

'King's Son, Sem (Priest), Mose-Djhuty'

This inscription identifies him as a 'Son of the King.'

Statuette of the Young Prince Thutmose

In the Louvre Museum there is a schist statuette of a prostrate young man grinding corn, wearing a short wig with the side-lock of youth, a kilt and a panther-skin. The panther skin identifies his as a Sem Priest and by tradition a position taken by the eldest son and heir to the throne:

s-HD, nsw sA, sm DHwty-ms

make-perish, king son, sem (priest) Mose-Djhuty

156

'Perished, the King's Son, the Sem (Priest of Ptah), Mose-Djhwty'

Again, this inscription takes note of his untimely death.

Death and Burial: unknown, disappears from record (dies) in year 27-33 of his father's reign.

▶

Family Tree: Amenhotep III, Akhenaten, Smenkhkara, Neferneferuaten, Tutankhamun and Ay

The Royal Amarna Families

Tuthmose IV + Queen Mutemwiya

Yuya + Tuya

Amenhotep III + Tiy

Anen

Ankhesenamun + **Akhenaten** + Nefertiti + Kiya + Meritaten + Sister

Ankhesnpaaten Setepenra Nefernerura Neferneferuaten-Tasherit Meketaten **Meritaten**

Meritaten + **Smenkhkara (2-3 yrs)**

Neferneferuaten (2 yrs)
(Female Ruler)

Tutankhaten (Tutankhamun) + Ankhesenpaaten (Ankhesenamun)

Ankhesenamun + **Ay** + Tey

HOTEP-AMUN

(AKH-EN-ATEN)

1353-1336 or 1351-1334 BC

Reign 17 yrs

sA ra (Htp-imn, nTr hqA wAst

son Ra (satisfied-Amun, god-riuler-Thebes)

Sa Ra (Hotep-Amun, Netjer Heqa Waset)

'Son of Ra, Amun is Satisfied, God Ruler of Thebes'

sA ra (Axt-itn)

son Ra (blessed spirit-Aten)

Sa Ra (Akhet-Aten)

'Son of Ra, Blessed Akh-Spirit of the Aten'

nsw bity (nfr-xpr-u-ra, wa-n-ra)

king-south-north (good-manifestations-Ra, sole-one of Ra)

Nesw Bity (Nefer-Kheper-u-Ra, Wa-en-Ra)

'King of Egypt, Good are the Creations of Ra, Sole On of Ra'

1390 BC	1380 BC	1370 BC	1360 BC	1350 BC	1340 BC	1330 BC
		Amenhotep III		Amenhotep IV - Akhenaten	N	Tutankhamun

Predecessor: Amenhotep III

Successor: Smenkhkara or Neferneferuaten

Consorts: Nefertiti, Kiya, Meritaten, Meketaten, Ankhesenamun, (Nebetah or Beketaten 'The Younger Lady')

Father: Amenhotep III

Mother: Queen Tiye

Children: Smenkhkara, Meritaten, Meketaten, Ankhesenamun, Neferneferuaten Tasherit, Neferneferura, Setepenra, Tutankhaten (Tutankhamun), Ankhesenpaaaten-ta-sherit

Died: 1336 or 1334 BC

Burial: Royal Tomb of Akhenaten (Amarna), Tomb 55?.

Name Change: Year 1-4 known as Amenhotep IV, Year 5-17 known as Akhenaten.

Reign: Amenhotep IV was the second son of Amenhotep III by his GRW Tiye. His elder brother Crown Prince Thutmose died

160

prematurely. He was crowned king at the age of sixteen at the temple of the god Amun at Karnak and like his father he married a lady of non-royal blood, Nefertiti, the daughter of the vizier Ay. Ay was a brother of Queen Tiye and a son of Yuia and Tjuia. Nefertiti's mother is not known, but she seems to have been brought up by another wife of Ay, named Tey.

Regnal Year 1
Amenhotep IV works on pylons at Karnak that his father started.
The pylons are dedicated to the Aten.
Meritaten is born.

Regnal Year 2
Work started in Thebes on 4 Aten temples.
Begins replacing the Amun name with Aten.
Depictions of Amenhotep IV become exaggerated.

Regnal Year 3
By this time, the first three daughters are born.

Regnal Year 4
The city of Akhetaten (Amarna) starts being built, and both the king and queen visit the site. His daughters Meketaten and Ankhesenpaaten born.

In the early years of his reign Amenhotep IV lived at Thebes with his wife Nefertiti and his six daughters.

Under is father Amenhotep III the power of the Amun priest hood had grown and so he made steps to curb it, this mission was taken up by his son Amenhotep IV who took more drastic steps to deviate their powers to the royal throne. This was done by introducing the new monotheistic cult of sun worship, the cult of the sun disc, the Aten.

The worship of the Aten sun disc as the provider of all life and light goes back to the Old Kingdom times, but during the reign of Amenhotep IV it would become the sole royal state cult. The protective rays of the Aten terminated in life giving hands holding the ankh hieroglyph, the sign for 'life.' Under the worship of the Aten there was no need for an intermediate priesthood, for the Aten was only accessible by the king.

Regnal Year 5

Changes name from Amenhotep to Akhenaten.
He says Aten is the only god.
He visits the site of the intended for the city of Akhetaten
and sets up some boundary stela.

Initially, Amenhotep IV built a temple to his god the Aten outside the east gate of the Temple of Amun at Karnak. Seeing the incompatibility of the two cults he closed the temples of Amun and took over their revenues. In year five he changed his name to Akhenaten, meaning the 'Akh-Spirit of the Aten' and started to build a new capital in Middle Egypt which was situated half-way between Memphis in the north and Thebes in the South:

Regnal Year 6

Central section of Akhetaten finished.

City created and dedicated this year.

Royal tomb started.

In year six Akhenaten moved to the new capital Akhet-Aten, meaning the 'Horizon of the Aten,' the site is known today as Amarna.

Regnal Year 8

Most of Akhetaten built, including the Great Temple enclosure.

Court moves to Akhetaten.

Inscribed a second group of stela at Akhetaten.

Regnal Year 9

Name of Aten is changed to remove references to any god except Ra.

In Year 9 of his reign, Akhenaten declared that Aten was not merely the supreme god, but the only god, and that he, Akhenaten, was the only intermediary between Aten and his people. He ordered the defacing of Amun's temples throughout Egypt and, in a number of instances, inscriptions of the plural 'gods' were also removed. In the new temples at Akhetaten, Aten was worshipped in the open sunlight, rather than in dark temple enclosures, as had been the previous custom. Akhenaten is also believed to have composed the Great Hymn to the Aten.

Regnal Year 10

Neferneferuaten is born.

Regnal Year 11

Neferneferura and Setepenra are born.

Regnal Year 12:

Great Durbar Celebration.
All six daughters are pictured for the last time.
Tiye visits Akhetaten and brings Baketaten with her.

Name of Amun still could be used in official inscriptions.
Meketaten dies (year 12 or year 13).

Regnal Year 13
Meketaten may have died this year.

Regnal Year 14
Last mention of Tiye on jar dockets at Akhetaten.
Nefertiti dies.
Meritaten is queen.

Regnal Year 15
Smenkhkara is possibly co-regent with Akhenaten.
Smenkhkara is married to Meritaten.
Akhenaten makes Ankhesenpaaten his consort.

Regnal Year 16
Last year Kiya's estate sends wine to Akhetaten.

Regnal Year 17
Akhenaten dies, probably after the grape harvest.

Death and Burial: The last dated appearance of Akhenaten and the Amarna family is in the tomb of Meryra II, and dates from the second month, year 12 of his reign. A recent find (2012) at a quarry north of Amarna establishes that Akhenaten and Nefertiti were still a royal couple just a year (Regnal Year 16) prior to Akhenaten's death. Akhenaten planned to relocate Egyptian burials on the East side of the Nile (sunrise) rather than on the West side (sunset), in the Royal Wadi in Akhetaten. His body was removed after the court returned to Thebes, and recent genetic tests have confirmed that the body found buried in tomb KV55 was the father of Tutankhamun, and is therefore 'most probably' Akhenaten, although this is in dispute.

It is generally accepted that Akhenaten himself died in Year 17 of his reign after a two or three year co-regency with Smenkhkara whose reign may have extended after Akhenaten's death. If Smenkhkare outlived Akhenaten, and became sole Pharaoh, he likely ruled Egypt for less than a year. The next successor was Neferneferuaten, a female Pharaoh who reigned in Egypt for two years and one month. She was, in turn, probably succeeded by Tutankhaten (Tutankhamun), with the country being administered by the chief vizier, and future Pharaoh, Ay.

Queen Nefertiti

NEFER-NEFERU-NEFER-II-TY

nfr-nfr-w, nfr-iity

beautiful-beauty-itn, beautiful-one come

Nefer-Neferu-Iten-Nerer-ii-ty

'Beautiful, Beauty of Aten, the Beautiful One who has Come'

Spouse: Amenhotep IV (Akhenaten)

Father: Ay? or King Tushratta of Mitanni?

Mother: Queen Juni of Mitanni?

Children: Meritaten, Meketaten, Ankhesenamun, Neferneferuaten Tasherit, Neferneferura, Setepenra

Born: 1370 BC

Died: 1330 BC

Lived: 40 yrs

Life: Neferneferuaten Nefertiti was the Great Royal Wife of Amenhotep IV (Akhenaten). Together with her husband they brought a revolution of art and cult in the form of the worship of the Aten to Egypt. It was during this time, the Amarna Period, that the splendour of Egypt reached its peak, in culture, wealth and artistic expression. It is believed that Nefertiti ruled briefly (2 or 3 yrs) as Neferneferuaten after her husband's death and before the accession of Tutankhamun.

Her titles include: 'Hereditary Princess, Great of Praises, Lady of Grace, Sweet of Love, Lady of the Two Lands, King's Great Wife, His Beloved, Lady of All Women' and 'Mistress of Upper and Lower Egypt.'

The most famous portrayal of her is a bust in the Berlin Museum. It was carried out by the sculptor Thutmose and exemplifies her beauty which is accentuated by her long neck; and as her name suggests, she certainly appears as the 'Beautiful, Beauty, the Beautiful One who has Come.'

Nefertiti's parentage is unknown, she may have been the daughter of Ay or Tushratta the King of Mitanni by his queen, Juni. Her six known daughters by Akhenaten:

Meritaten: born year 1

Meketaten: born year 4

Ankhesenpaaten: became known as Ankhesenamun, Queen of Tutankhamun.

Neferneferuaten Tasherit: possibly became Pharaoh Neferneferuaten

Neferneferura: born year 9

Setepenra: born year 11

Death and Burial: Nefertiti probably died soon after her husband's death in year 17 of his reign. Her mummy has not been found.

Queen Kiya

KY-IA

ky-iA

Ky-ia

Spouse: Amenhotep IV (Akhenaten)

Father: unknown

Mother: unknown

Children: unnamed daughter

Life: Queen Kiya was one of the wives of Akhenaten, she may have had Mitannian origins, during the middle years of his reign she bore him a daughter (unnamed). She may have been the Mitannian prince Tadukhipa, daughter of Tushratta. Kiya was given the titles 'The Favourite' and 'The Greatly Beloved.'

Death and Burial: Kiya disappears from the records during the last third of the king's reign. It is uncertain whether she simply died or fell from grace and was exiled; her mummy and tomb are unknown.

Meritaten

Princess, Queen and Pharaoh

(Female King Neferneferuaten)

MERET-ATEN

sA ra (nfr-nfrw-itn)

son Ra (beautiful-beauty-Aten)

Sa Ra, Nefer-neferu-Iten

'Son of Ra, Beautiful Beauty of the Aten'

mrt-iten

Meret-Aten

'Beloved of the Aten'

Spouse: Smenkhkara and possibly her father Amenhotep IV (Akhenaten)

Father: Amenhotep IV (Akhenaten)

Mother: Queen Nefertiti

Siblings: sisters: Meketaten, Ankhesenpaaten, Neferneferuaten Tasherit, Neferneferura, and Setepenra

Life: Meritaten was the eldest daughter of Akhenaten and his Great Royal Wife Nefertiti. She is known to have the title of 'Great Royal Wife,' she may have married her father later in his reign and assumed this title, but it is also recorded that Meritaten was Great Royal Wife to Smenkhkare (Tomb of Meryra II in Akhet-Aten). She is listed alongside King Akhenaten and King Neferneferuaten as 'Great Royal Wife' on a box from the tomb of Tutankhamen. Letters written to Akhenaten from foreign rulers make reference to Meritaten as 'mistress of the house.'

During Akhenaten's reign she was the most frequently depicted and mentioned of the six daughters. Her figure appears on paintings in temples, tombs, and private chapels. She is shown not only on the pictures showing the family life of the pharaoh, which were typical of the Amarna Period, but on official ceremonies too.

According to some scholars, Smenkhkare ruled together with Meritaten. After a short co-regency with his father Akhenaten, Smenkhkara ruled with Meritaten, but in the year following Akhenaten's death Smenkhkare himself died. It is possible that Meritaten assumed the throne for herself as the female king Neferneferuaten. Neferneferuaten is assigned a reign of 2 years and 1 month and is placed in Manetho's account as the immediate predecessor of Rathothis, who is believed to be Tutankhamun.

Death and Burial: It is not known what happened to Meritaten. There are no known funerary goods inscribed with her name that have ever surfaced. She seems to have disappeared from the scene at roughly the same time as her husband Smenkhkara. There is some speculation that both Meritaten and Smenkhkara may have died due to a plague that seems to have been ravaging the region at that time.

Some believe that Meritaten did survive and took the throne as Neferneferuaten and either ruled until her death or served as regent for the young Tutankhamen.

(Meritaten) Female Pharaoh Neferneferuaten:

sA ra (iten-nfr-nfr-w)

Sa Ra (Nefer-neferu Iten)

'Son Ra (Beautiful-Beauty of Aten)'

Princess Meketaten

𓇋𓏏𓇳𓌰𓏏𓅱

mkt-iten

protect-Aten

Meket-Aten

'Protected by the Aten'

Father: Akhenaten

Mother: Nefertiti

Siblings: her sisters Meritaten, Ankhesenpaaten, Neferneferuaten Tasherit, Neferneferura, and Setepenra

Life: Meketaten was the second eldest daughter of Akhenaten and Nefertiti. She was probably born in year 4 of Akhenaten's reign. Although little is known about her, she is frequently depicted with her sisters accompanying her royal parents in the first two thirds of Akhenaten's seventeen-year reign. She had an older sister named Meritaten and four younger sisters named Ankhesenpaaten, Neferneferuaten Tasherit, Neferneferura and Setepenra. Tutankhaten (later Tutankhamun) was her half-brother.

Meketaten moved to the new capital city Akhetaten with her family when she was still a small child. Meketaten was depicted with her parents and sisters at Amarna attending a ceremony dating to year 12 (the Reception of Foreign Tributes).

Death and Burial: Meketaten died in year 14 of her father's (Akhenaten) reign. She may have died from a plague or in childbirth. Fragments of Meketaten's sarcophagus were found in the Royal Tomb of Akhenaten at Amarna.

Princess Neferneferuaten Ta Sherit

NEFER-NEFER-U-ITEN TA-SHERET

Neferneferuaten Ta Sherit on the right of her sister Neferneferura

nfr-nfr-w-iten-tA-Srt

beauty-beauties-Aten-the-younger

Nefer-nefer-u-Iten-Ta-Sheret

'The Most Beautiful One of the Aten - The Younger'

Consort: her father Akhenaten

Father: Akhenaten

Mother: Nefertiti

Siblings: her sisters Meritaten, Beketaten, Ankhesenpaaten, Neferneferura, and Setepenra

Life: Princess Neferneferuaten - The Younger (Tasherit) was the fourth daughter of Pharaoh Akhenaten and his Great Royal Wife

174

Nefertiti. She was born between year 8 and 9 of her father's reign and was probably born at Akhetaten (Amarna) and had three older sisters named, Meritaten, Beketaten, and Ankhesenpaaten and two younger sisters named Neferneferura, and Setepenra. She is depicted at the Durbar in year 12 in the tomb of the Overseer of the royal quarters Meryra II in Amarna. Akhenaten and Nefertiti are shown seated in a kiosk, receiving tribute from foreign lands.

Three daughters of Akhenaten at the Year 12 Durbar: from rig to left: Neferneferuaten (Ta Sherit), Neferneferura and Setepenra.

In the scene above Neferneferuaten has the titles:

nsw sAt, n Xt.f, mr-t.f, nfr-nfr-w-itn

king daughter, of body.his, beloved.his, beauty-beautiful

Nesew Sat, en khet.ef, meret.ef, Neferneferuaten

'King's Daughter, of His Body, His Beloved, Beauty of Beauties of the Aten'

175

Death and Burial: It is unknown what became of Neferneferuaten - The Younger (Tasherit), but she was shown with her sisters Meritaten and Ankhesenpaaten mourning the death of possibly Meketaten in year 14 in the Royal Tomb in Amarna.

Princess Neferneferura

NEFER-NEFER-U-RA

𓇳𓏥𓄤𓄤𓄤𓄤

nfr-nfr-w-ra

beauty-beauties-Ra

Nefer-nefer-u-ra

'Beauty of Beauties of Ra'

Father: Akhenaten

Mother: Nefertiti

Siblings: her sisters Meritaten, Beketaten, Ankhesenpaaten, Neferneferuaten, and Setepenra

Life: Princess Neferneferura was the fifth of six known daughters of Pharaoh Akhenaten and Great Royal Wife Nefertiti. She was born in or before the 8th regnal year of her father Akhenaten in the city of Akhetaten. She had four older sisters named Meritaten, Meketaten, Ankhesenpaaten and Neferneferuaten Tasherit, as well as a younger sister named Setepenra.

In the scene of the three daughters of Akhenaten at the Year 12 Durbar, Neferneferura is given the titles:

𓇓𓅭 𓈖𓏏𓆄𓆑 𓌸𓂋𓏏𓆑 𓇳𓄤𓄤𓄤𓄤

nsw sAt, n Xt.f, mrt.f, nfr-nfr-w-ra

king daughter, of body.his, beloved.his, beautiful-beauty-Ra

Nesw Sat, en khet.ef, meret.ef, Nefer-nefer-u-ra

'King's Daughter, of His Body,

His Beloved, Beauty of Beauties of Ra'

Princess Setepenra

SETEP-EN-RA

stp-n-ra

chosen-of-Ra

Setep-en-Ra

'Chosen of Ra'

Father: Akhenaten

Mother: Nefertiti

Siblings: her sisters Meritaten, Beketaten, Ankhesenpaaten, Neferneferuaten, and Neferneferura

Life: Princess Setepenra was the sixth and last daughter of Pharaoh Akhenaten and his chief queen Nefertiti.

In the scene of the three daughters of Akhenaten at the Year 12 Durbar, Setepenra is given the titles:

nsw sAt, n Xt.f, mrt.f, stp-n-ra

king daughter, of body.his, beloved.his, chosen-of-Ra

Nesw Sat, en khet.ef, meret.ef, Setep-en-ra

179

'King's Daughter, of his Body, his Beloved, Chosen of Ra'

Death and Burial: It is probable that Setepenra predeceased Neferneferura, and it is likely that Setepenra died around Year 13 or 14, before she reached her sixth birthday. It is possible that she was interred in the Royal Tomb at Amarna.

Princess Ankhesenpaaten Tasherit

ANKH-ES-EN-PA-ITEN TA-SHERET

anx-s-n-pA-itn tA-Srt

life-she-of-Aten the-younger

Ankh-es-en-Iten Ta-Sheret

'She is the Life of the Aten, The Young One'

Father: Akhenaten?

Mother: Ankhesenpaaten?

Siblings: her sisters Meritaten, Beketaten, Neferneferuaten, Neferneferura and Setepenra.

Life: Princess Ankhesenpaaten Tasherit was possibly the young daughter of the Great Royal Wife Ankhesenpaaten, meaning Akhenaten was probably her father. Assuming this is correct then she must have been born towards the very end of Akhenaten's reign. Since Ankhesenpaaten was born around the 5th year of her father's reign, the earliest year she could have had a child was around Year 16 of his reign.

An inscription on a block found at Hermopolis gives the name and titles of Ankhesenpaaten Tasherit, born of Ankhesenpaaten:

nsw sAt, n Xt.f, mrt.f, anx-s-n-pA-itn, tA-Srt

king daughter, of body.his, beloved.his, life-she-of-itn, the-younger

181

'Nesw Sat, en khet.ef, meret.ef, Ankh-es-en-pa-Iten, Ta-sheret

'King's Daughter, of His body, His Beloved,

She is the Life of the Aten, The Young One'

ms n, nsw sAt, n Xt.f, anx-s-n-pA-itn

born of, king's daughter, of body.his, life-she-of-the-Aten

'Mes en, Nesw Sat, en khet.ef, Ankh-es-en-pa-Iten'

'Born of the King's Daughter, of His body, Ankhesenpaaten (She is the Life of the Aten)'

Djeserkheperu

S-MENKH-KA-RA DJESER-KHEPER-U

ANKH-KHEPER-U-RA

1335 - 1334 BC

Reign Co-regency 2 yrs, Sole 1 yr

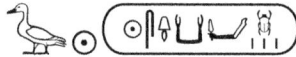

sA ra (s-mnx-kA-ra, Dsr-xpr-w)

son Ra (make-potent-soul-Ra, godly-manifestations)

Sa Ra (S-menkh-ka-Ra, Djeser-kheper-u)

'Son of Ra, Made Potent the Ka of Ra, Holy of Forms'

nswt bity (anx-xpr-w-ra)

king-south-north (living-manifestations-Ra)

Nesw Bity (Ankh-kheper-u-Ra)

'King of the South and North, Living Manifestations of Ra'

183

Predecessor: Akhenaten

Successor: Neferneferuaten

Consort: Meritaten

Father: Akhenaten

Mother: Nefertiti

Siblings: his sister and consort Meritaten, Meketaten, Ankhesenamun, Neferneferuaten Tasherit, Neferneferura, Setepenra, Tutankhaten (Tutankhamun), Ankhesenpaaaten-ta-sherit

Life: Pharaoh Smenkhkara ruled Egypt probably and initially was in a co-regency with Akhenaten (at the end of Akhenaten's reign) for most of the period of his rule which was only 2-3 yrs. Smenkhkara's origin and identity remain among the unresolved issues of the Amarna period.

The elusive Smenkhkare appears only at the very end of Akhenaten's reign in a few monuments at the royal capital of Akhetaten (Amarna). He shares the same coronation name, Ankh-kheperu-ra, with another royal individual called Neferneferuaten (part of the expanded name of Nefertiti). Since coronation names are generally unique to one individual, it has been suggested that Smenkhkare is in fact Nefertiti herself, raised to kingly status to share the throne with her husband at the end of his life.

Death and Burial: In one tomb at Akhetaten, Smenkhkare is shown with the eldest daughter of Akhenaten, Meritaten, then elevated to the status of queen; whether her new office represents an actual marriage or simply an honorary status conferred on her remains unclear. The only dated document of Smenkhkara's reign is a graffito from a Theban tomb, which notes his third regnal year.

Cranial and serological analyses indicated that the mummy of a male discovered in tomb KV 55 of the Valley of the Kings has affinities close to those of Tutankhamen. Some scholars accepted the identification of the remains as Smenkhkara's on the basis of fragmentary inscriptions in the tomb, concluding that Smenkhkare and Tutankhamen were brothers who succeeded Akhenaten in turn. However, other scholars suggested that the mummy might belong to Akhenaton himself. Subsequent tests run by Egypt's Supreme Council of Antiquities on a number of royal mummies indicated that the unidentified mummy from KV 55 was the father of Tutankhamen and the son of Amenhotep III, a lineage that matches that of Akhenaten.

Nenferneferuaten

(Female Pharaoh)

NEFER-NEFER-U-ATEN

1334-1332 BC

Reigned: 2 yrs

sA ra (nfr-nfr-w-itn)

son Ra (beauty-beauties-Aten)

Sa Ra (Nefer-nefer-u-Iten)

'Son of Ra, Beautiful One of Beauties of the Aten'

nsw bity (anx-xpr-w-ra)

king-south-north (life-manifestations-Ra)

Nesw Bity (Ankh-kheper-u-Ra)

'King of Egypt, Living Manifestations of Ra)

1390 BC	1380 BC	1370 BC	1360 BC	1350 BC	1340 BC	1330 BC
		Amenhotep III		Amenhotep IV - Akhenaten	N	Tutankhamun

Predecessor: Smenkhkara? Akhenaten?

Successor: Tutankhamun

Consort: if she was Nefertiti: Akhenaten; if she was Meritaten: Smenkhkara

Father: ?

Mother: ?

Life: Neferneferuaten was a woman who reigned as pharaoh after Akhenaten and probably Smenkhkara. Her gender is confirmed by feminine traces occasionally found in the name and by the epithet Akhet-en-hyes 'Effective for her husband,' incorporated into one version of her second cartouche. She is to be distinguished from the king who used the name Ankh-kheper-u-ra Smenkhkara-Djeser Kheperu but without epithets appearing in either cartouche.

A number of items in Tutankhamun's tomb were originally intended for **Neferneferuaten**, but of particular interest is a box (Carter 001k) inscribed with the following:

#1 Line of text with the name and titles of **Meritaten**:

'King's Great Wife (**Merit-Aten**) May she Live Forever'

#2 Line of text with the name and titles of **<u>Neferneferuaten</u>**:

King of Egypt, Lord of the Two Lands

(Ankh-kheper-u-ra, Mery-nefer-kheper-ra)

King's Son, Lord of Crowns (**Nefer-nefer-u-aten**, Mery-wa-en-ra)

#3 Line of text with the name and titles of **Akhenaten**

'King of Egypt, Living in Truth, Lord of Crowns (**Akhen-aten**) Great in His Duration

In the above inscription (**#2**) **Neferneferuaten** has the added name of **Merywaenra** meaning 'Beloved One of Ra.'

TUT-ANKH-ATEN

TUT-ANKH-AMUN

1332-1323 BC

Reigned: 9 yrs

1340 BC	1330 BC	1320 BC	1310 BC	1300 BC
N	Tutankhamun	Ay	Horemeb	

(Amarna Yr 1-3)

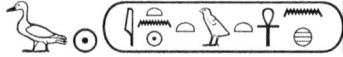

sA-ra (twt-anx-itnn)

son Ra (image-living-Aten)

Sa Ra (Tut-ankh-Aten)

'Son of Ra, Living Image of the Aten'

(Thebes Yr 3-9)

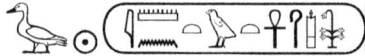

sA ra (twt-anx-imn, HqA iwn Sma

son Ra (image-living-Amun, ruler pillar-town southern)

Sa Ra (Twt-ankh-Imun, Heqa Iwnw Shema)

'Son of Ra, Living Image of Amun, Ruler of Upper Heliopolis'

nswt bity (nb-xpr-u-ra)

king-south-north (lord-manifestations-Ra)

Neswt Bity (Neb-kheper-u-ra)

'King of Egypt, Lord of Manifestations of Ra'

Predecessor: Neferneferuaten or Smenkhkare

Successor: Ay

Consort: Ankhesenpaaten (Amarna)-Ankhesenamun (Thebes)

Father: Akhenaten

Mother: 'The Younger Lady' (probably Nebetah or Beketaten)

Children: Two stillborn daughters

Born: 1341 BC

Died: 1323 BC aged 18 years

Burial: KV62

Life: Tutankhamun is one of the most famous kings of ancient Egypt; his tomb (KV62) was found intact in 1922 by Howard Carter under the sponsorship of Lord Carnarvon. The discovery and splendour of his gold filled tomb made world headlines.

Tutankhamun was the son of the infamous Pharaoh Amenhotep IV (**Akhenaten**) (mummy KV55) and one of his wives named 'The Younger Lady' (a name given to a mummy found in KV25, the tomb of Amenhotep II). DNA testing of this mummy 'The Younger Lady' was shown in February 2010 to be a woman, the mother of Tutankhamun, and the daughter of Amenhotep III and Tiye (making her both the sister and wife of Akhenaten). Her name, however, remains unknown, leaving open the possibility that she is likely to be either **Nebetah** or **Beketaten**.

His family tree: from the family tree it can be seen that Tutankhamun's grandfather was Amenhotep III and that is great grandfather was Thutmose IV. His wife, Ankhesenamun, was his half-sister (Same father Akhenaton, different mothers), who's mother was Nefertiti.

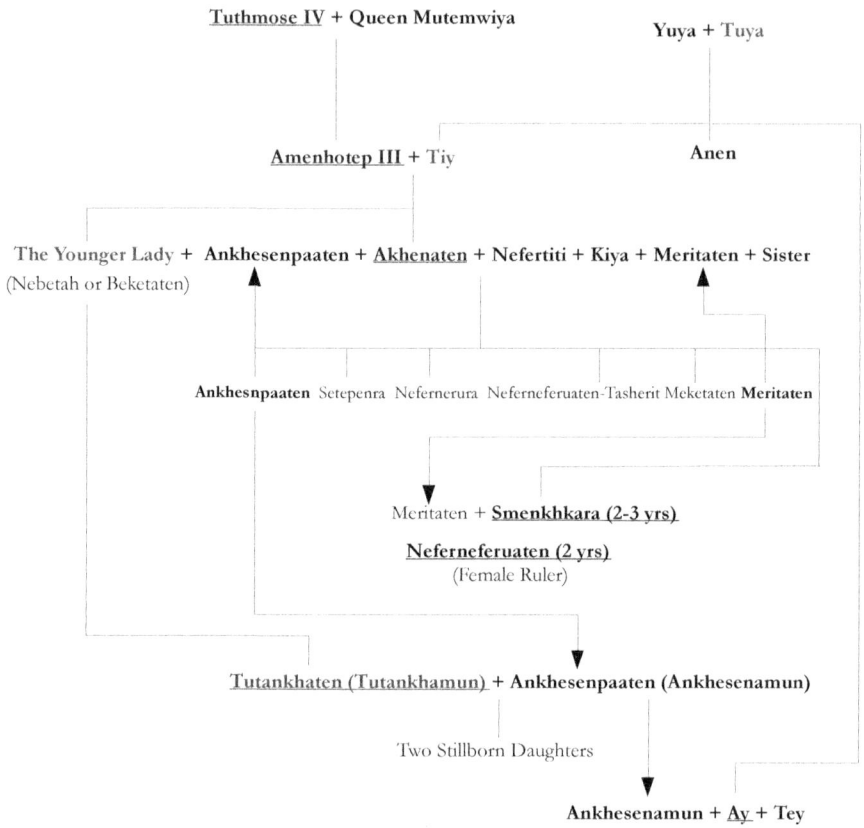

Tuthmose IV + Queen Mutemwiya

Yuya + Tuya

Amenhotep III + Tiy

Anen

The Younger Lady + Ankhesenpaaten + Akhenaten + Nefertiti + Kiya + Meritaten + Sister
(Nebetah or Beketaten)

Ankhesnpaaten Setepenra Nefernerura Neferneferuaten-Tasherit Meketaten Meritaten

Meritaten + Smenkhkara (2-3 yrs)
Neferneferuaten (2 yrs)
(Female Ruler)

Tutankhaten (Tutankhamun) + Ankhesenpaaten (Ankhesenamun)

Two Stillborn Daughters

Ankhesenamun + Ay + Tey

Life at Akhetaten (Amarna): Tutankhamun was probably born at Amarna and was given the birth (Sa Ra) name of Tutankhaten (The Living image of the Aten). He was 9 or 10 years old when he ascended the throne and married his half-sister Ankhesenpaaten. His Aten name is on his throne chair and was probably used at Amarna until his name change and move to Thebes under the restored cult of Amun. His name and that of his wife's were changed to Tutankhamun and Ankhesenamun. They had two daughters who were both stillborn.

The two main advisors to the young king were the Vizier Ay and the General of the Army, Horemheb, who both became pharaohs after the death of Tutankhamun.

Life at Thebes: In year 3 of his reign, Tutankhamun reversed the changes made during his father's reign. He ended the worship of the god Aten and restored the god Amun. The capital was moved back to Thebes and the city of Akhetaten abandoned. This is when he changed his name to Tutankhamun, 'Living image of Amun', reinforcing the restoration of the god Amun. It is probable that much of the influence for this change back to the traditional Amun cult came from his senior advisors Ay and Horemheb. As part of his restoration, the king initiated building projects, in particular at Thebes and Karnak, where he dedicated a temple to Amun.

At the temple of Soleb in Nubia built by his grandfather Amenhotep III he inscribed two red granite lions installed there with the declaration:

smAAwy mnw, n it.i

restored monuments, of father.my

'...restored the monuments of my father (Amenhotep III)'

Death and Burial: There is much conjecture and theory about the death of Tutankhamun and most involve death by conspiracy assassination, accident or disease, but it is believed that genetic defects arising from his parents being siblings, complications from a broken leg and his suffering from malaria, together caused his death.

Tutankhamun was buried in a tomb that was small relative to his status. His death may have occurred unexpectedly, before the completion of a grander royal tomb, so that his mummy was buried in a tomb intended for someone else, maybe the Vizier Ay, who took over Tutankhamun's original tomb (WV23) which has similar decoration.

King Tutankhamun's mummy still rests in his tomb in the Valley of the Kings (KV62).

Princess & Queen

Ankhesenpaaten - Ankhesenamun

ANKH-ES-EN-PA-ATEN

ANKH-ES-EN-AMUN

Ankhesenpaaten and Tutankhaten under the rays of the Aten.
A touching scene on his gold throne chair

Reign: 1332-1323 BC
9 yrs

anx-s-n-pA-itn

life-se-of-the-Aten

Ankh-es-en-pa-Iten

'She is the Life of the Aten'

anx-s-n-imn

life-she-of-Amun

Ankh-es-en-Imun

'She is the Life of Amun'

Spouses: Akhenaten (her father), Tutankhaten-Tutankhamun (her half brother) and Ay (the Vizier)

Father: Akhenaten

Mother: Nefertiti

Children: Two unborn daughters and probably Ankhesenpaaten Tasherit

Siblings: Smenkhkara, Meritaten, Meketaten, Neferneferuaten Tasherit, Neferneferura, Setepenra, Tutankhaten-Tutankhamun.

Born: 1248 BC

Died: 1322 BC aged 26 yrs

Burial: possibly KV21

Life: Princess Ankhesenpaaten was born in Thebes in Year 4 of her father's (Amenhotep IV-Akhenaten) reign by his Great Royal Wife Nefertiti. This was the year before the family moved to Amarna (Akhetaten). In Year 15 of Akhenaten's reign she becomes his Royal Consort. Ankhesenpaaten is probably the mother of the young princess Ankhesenpaaten Ta Sherit (The Younger) by her father and husband Akhenaten. It is thought she was 12 years old when she gave birth to her daughter.

After her father's death and the short reigns of Smenkhkare and Neferneferuaten, she became the wife of Tutankhaten. Following their marriage, the couple honoured the god Amun and restored his cult at Thebes. They demonstrated their allegiance to the cult of Amun by changing their names to Tutankhamun and Ankhesenamun. The couple appear to have had two stillborn daughters. As Tutankhamun's only known wife was Ankhesenamun, it is highly likely the foetuses found in Tutankhamun's tomb are her daughters. Sometime in the ninth year of Tutankhamun's reign, when he was at about the age of eighteen, he died suddenly, leaving Ankhesenamun alone without an heir. She was aged twenty-one when he died. Shortly after Tutankhamun's death she marries the Vizier Ay who acted as the Sem Priest (Chosen Son and Heir) at her husband's funeral. Vizier Ay's marriage to Ankhesenamun and acting out the role of Sem Priest enabled him to legitimize his claim to the throne.

There is evidence that before her marriage to Ay, in fear and desperation to avoid marrying a 'commoner,' she sent a letter to the Hittite King Suppiluliuma I seeking his help in providing her with a consort from one of his sons. She writes:

'*My husband has died and I have no son. They say about you that you have many sons. You might give me one of your sons to become my husband. I would not wish to take one of my subjects as a husband... I am afraid.*'

Suppiluliuma was surprised by the request, understandably, he was wary, and sent an envoy to investigate, but by so doing, he missed his chance to bring Egypt into his empire. He eventually did send one of his sons, Zannanza, but the prince died, perhaps murdered, en route.

Shortly after the coronation of Ay to the throne, Ankhesenamun disappears from the records; Ay is only depicted with his senior wife Tey in his tomb.

Death and Burial: unknown

Tomb of Tutankhamun

The Art & Hieroglyphic Inscriptions

(King's Valley 62)

North wall of the burial chamber

The large painting on the north wall shows Tutankhamun in three separate scenes. On the right the former Vizier Ay, now as Pharaoh and acting Sem Priest is wearing the blue war crown and dressed in the traditional leopard skin (the uniform of a Sem Priest), he performs the opening of the mouth ceremony on the deceased Osiris King Tutankhamun. This ceremony was usually performed by the deceased's son and heir, in this case the following king, Ay performs the right which secures his position as the next pharaoh.

The middle scene shows Tutankhamun as the living king being greeted by the goddess Nut into the realm of the gods. In the left scene wearing the Nemes headdress Tutankhamun is followed behind by his ka, his spiritual double, and is welcomed by Osiris, king of the dead.

Right scene – North Wall

Left register over Tutankhamun

nTr nfr, nb tAwy, nb xaw (ra-xpr-w-nb)

god good, lord two-lands, lord appearances KNS (kheper-u-nb-Ra)

'The good god, lord of the two-lands and lord of appearances, King of Upper and Lower Egypt, Neb-kheper-u-ra'

Right register over Ay

nTr nfr, nb tAwy, nb ir xt, nsw-bit (ra-xpr*-u)

god good, lord two-lands, lord doing things, KNS (Ra-kheperu)

'The good god, lord of the Two-Lands, lord of doing things (Kheper-kheper-u-ra)

* Note: in Ay's cartouche the plural (**w**) of **xpr-w** is expressed by the repetition of three signs, in other places his name reads: 'Kheper-kheper-u-ra.'

Middle scene north wall

Right register over Tutankhamun

nb tAwy (ra-xpr-w-nb) di anx DtA HH

lord two-lands (Ra-kheper-u-neb) given life eternity forever

'Lord of the Two-Lands, Neb-kheper-u-ra, may he be given life eternal forever'

nwt, nbt pt, (H)nwt nTrw, ir.s, nyny, n ms n.s

Nut, lady heaven, mistress gods, make.she, do-homage, of born of.her

di.s, snb anx, (r-unclear).k, anx (rnp-unclear) Dt(A)

give.she, health life, (to?.you) life (years?) forever

'Nut, Lady of Heaven, mistress of the gods, may she make homage to (him) born of her, may she give health and life to (?) you, life for all time (?)'

Left scene – north wall

Right register – above Tutankhamun's Ka – identifying his ka name

Hr wADt, ka-nxt, ka

Horus Cobra-goddess, [Bull-strong], Soul-Double

'Horus and Wadjet, [Victorious Bull], Soul-double'

nsw spt* n, xntt bHdt

king of Abydos, foremost (of) Edfu-temple

'King of Abydos, foremost of Edfu Temple?'

* Nome of Abydos

The South Wall

The south wall depicts the deceased Tutankhamun, who is wearing the **khat** headdress, being welcomed into the realm of the gods. On his right and facing him is the goddess Hathor who is holding the sign of life, the ankh, to his nose, the seat (breath) of life. To his immediate left is the jackal headed god, Anubis, the god of embalming. Anubis greets Tutankhamun by placing his left hand upon his shoulder. To the left of Anubis stands the goddess Isis ready to greet Tutankhamun to the underworld with the gift of water, the water is represented by the the **mu** sign which she holds in each hand. Behind her, sit three minor deities.

The south wall (left) – West wall (right)
Register above Hathor

Ht-Hr, nbt pt, Hry-tp DAtt imnt
Hat-hor, lady heaven, chieftan estate west
'Hathor, lady of heaven, chief of the estate of the west'

The west side of the Nile, where the sun sets to the underworld, is the burial necropolis of tombs and temples. Register above Tutankhamun's head

nTr nfr (ra-xpr-w-nb) di anx Dt(A) HH
god good (Ra-kheper-u-nb) given life eternal forever
'The good god, Neb-kheper-u-ra, may he be given eternal life forever'

inpw, xntt imnt, nTr nfr, im(?)t, nb pt

Inpu, foremost west, god good, who-is-in?, lord heaven

'Anubis, foremost of the west, lord of heaven'

Part of the West Wall

This scene depicts twelve baboon deities of the twelve hours of the night (6 shown) through which the solar bark and the king must travel through before reaching rebirth at dawn.

The top register shows the sung god Khepri in a solar bark, either side are two worshiping deities, identified by the inscription above their heads as Osiris:

dwA xpr dwA

'adore Khepri adore'

wsir xpr wsir
'Osiris Khepri Osiris'

The names of the baboon deities: Read right to left and down: Note: the lighter text written in red is read first followed by the darker text written in black:

Hkn m bs-f
exult as flame-his

'Extol (him) as Besef'
HEKEN-EM-BESEF

nis m bs-f
'Call (him) as Besef'
NIS-EM-BESEF

hTty
'Hetjety'
HETJETY

ib wi
heart come

hnw
jubilate
'Come, heart rejoice'
IB-WI-HENU

pATT
'Patjetj'
PATJETJ

bsy
'Besy'
BESY

Vizier & Pharaoh

Ay It-Netjer Kheperkheperura

IY IT-NETJER

KHEPER-KHEPER-U-RA

1323-1319 BC

Reign: 4 yrs

sA ra (it-nTr, iy)

son Ra (father-god, Iy)

Sa Ra (It-ntjer, Iy)

'Son of Ra, Father of the God, Ay'

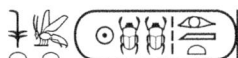

nswt bity (xpr-xpr-w-ra, ir-mAat)

king-south-north (existing-manifestations-Ra, doing-truth)

Nesw Bity (Kepher-khepr-u-ra, Ir-Maat)

'King of Egypt, Existing Manifestations of Ra, Doer of Truth)

1340 BC	1330 BC	1320 BC	1310 BC	1300 BC
	N Tutankhamun Ay		Horemeb	

Predecessor: Tutankhamun

Successor: Horemheb

Consort: Ankhesenamun, Great Royal Wife Tey

Father: Yuia

Mother: Tjuia

Siblings: his sister Queen Tiye, his brother Anen (Prophet of Amun)

Died: 1319 or 1323 BC

Burial: WV23

Life: Ay was the penultimate Pharaoh of the 18th Dynasty, he succeeded the boy king Tutankhamun after his death and married Tutankhamun's wife Ankhesenamun who was about 26 years of age. As vizier he was the power behind the throne during the reign of Tutankhamun and probably had a great influence on his life. It was Ay who was possibly the driving force behind the change from the monotheism of Amenhotep and Akhenaten back to the worship of the old gods at Amun's cult centre, Thebes. Soon into his reign he took Tey as his Great Royal Wife and his consort Ankhesenamun disappears from the scene.

Ay is reasoned to be the son of Yuia, who served as a member of the priesthood of Min at Akhmin as well as superintendent of herds in this city, and wife Tjuia. Yuya was an influential nobleman at the royal court of Amenhotep III who was given the rare privilege of having a tomb built for his use in the royal Valley of the Kings presumably because he was the father of Tiye, Amenhotep's chief Queen. During the reign of Akhenaten, Ay had achieved the title of 'Overseer of All the Horses of His Majesty,' the highest rank in the elite charioteering division of the army, which was just below the rank of General. Other titles listed in this tomb include 'Fan-bearer on the Right Side of the King, 'Acting Scribe of the King, beloved by him, and God's Father.' The Fan-bearer on the Right Side of the King' was a very important position, and is viewed as showing that the bearer had the 'ear' of the ruler.

Ay ruled Egypt in his own right for only four years. During this period, he consolidated the return to the old religious ways that he had initiated as senior advisor and constructed a mortuary temple at Medinet Habu for his own use.

Death and Burial: On is coronation Ay was already an old man and in view of his age it is of little wonder that his reign lasted only 4 years. Ay was interred in tomb Western Valley 23 which may have originally been prepared for Tutankhamun. His mummy has not been identified.

Queen Tey

TIY

tiy

Tiye

Consort: Pharaoh Ay It-Netjer

Children: none known

Life: Tey was the wife of Kheperkheperura Ay, who was the penultimate pharaoh of Ancient Egypt's 18th Dynasty. She was also the wet nurse of Queen Nefertiti. Her husband, Ay filled an important role in the courts of several pharaohs (Amenhotep III, Akhenaten and Tutankhamen) before ascending the throne himself, as the male line of the royal family had became extinct.

Queen Tey held the title of 'Great Royal Wife' of Ay; she also held the titles of: 'Hereditary Princess, Great of Praises, Lady of The Two Lands, Great King's Wife, his beloved, and Mistress of Upper and Lower Egypt.

Death and Burial: Tiye was probably interred in her husband's tomb WV23 where she is portrayed. Her mummy has not been found.

HER-EM-HEB

1306 - 1292 BC

Reigned: 14 yrs

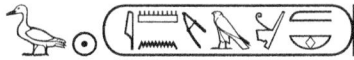

sA ra (Hr-m-Hb, mri-imn)

son Ra (Horus-in-festival, beloved Amun)

Sa Ra (Her-em-heb, meri-Amun)

'Son of Ra, Horus in Festival, Beloved of Amun'

nswt bity (Dsr-xpr-u-ra, stp-n-ra)

king-south-north (sacred-manifestations-Ra, chosen-of-Ra)

Nesw Bity (Djeser-kheper-u-ra, Setep-en-ra)

'King of the South and North, Sacred Manifestations of Ra, Chosen of Ra'

1340 BC	1330 BC	1320 BC	1310 BC	1300 BC
	N Tutankhamun Ay		Horemeb	

Predecessor: Ay

Successor: Ramesses I

Consort: Amenia, Mutnedjmet

Father: ?

Mother: ?

Children: none

Siblings: ?

Died: 1292 BC

Burial: KV57

Reign: Horemheb was the last king of the 18th Dynasty. Little is known about his background except that he was a commoner and came from\Herakleopolis Magna and that he was the commander in chief of the army during the reigns of Tutankhamun and Ay. After the death of Ay and with the lack of an heir to the throne he declared himself king and legitimized this move by taking a sister of Nefertiti, a lady called Mutnedjmet as his royal wife. Horemheb's first wife was a noble lady named Amenia; she seems to have died during his reign and was buried in his Memphite tomb alongside his second wife Mutnedjmet.

Horemheb must have been middle aged when he came to the throne and immediately set about repairing and re-opening the temples and bringing back the priesthood of Amun. He demolished monuments of Akhenaten and usurped monuments of Ay and Tutankhamun.

Horemheb's titles include: 'Commander in Chief of the Army, Hereditary Prince, Fan Bearer on the Right Side of the King and Sole Companion.'

Death and Burial: Horemheb had made preparations for his burial before he became king, his private tomb was at Saqqara, but as Pharaoh he commissioned a new tomb in the Valley of the Kings (KV57). Horemheb's mummy has not been found.

Horemheb presumably remained childless during his reign since he appointed his vizier Paramesse as his successor, who would assume the throne as Ramesses I.

Armenia

(First Wife of Horemheb)

imn-iA

Armenia

Consort: Horemheb, her husband before his coronation.

Life: Amenia was an Egyptian noble woman and the first wife of Horemheb. Very little is known about her, and she seems to have died during the reign of Ay or early during the reign of Tutankhamun, before Horemheb ruled as pharaoh.

Death and Burial: Amenia was buried in the Memphite tomb of Horemheb in the upper suite in shaft IV, alongside his second wife Mutnedjmet.

Queen Mutnedjmet

mwt-nDmt

mother (Mut)-sweet

Mutnedjmet

'Sweet Mother'

Consort: Horemheb

Siblings: possibly she was a sister of Nefertiti

Life: Mutnedjmet was the Great Royal Wife of Horemheb and possibly the sister of Nefertiti. Her royal titles include: 'King's Great Wife, Great of Praises, Lady of Grace, Sweet of Love, Mistress of Upper and Lower Egypt, Songstress of Hathor and Songstress of Amun.'

Death and Burial: Mutnedjmet died soon after Year 13 of her husband's reign in her mid-40s. Her mummy was found in King Horemheb's unused Memphite tomb along with the mummy of a still-born, premature infant. She appears to have been buried in the Memphite tomb of Horemheb, alongside his first wife Amenia.

APPENDIX

Royal Titles

#1 Hereditary Prince (Iry-pat)

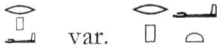

[hieroglyphs] var. [hieroglyphs]

r-pat, iry-pat 'Hereditary Prince, Prince, Noble, Heir (masculine).'

In the New Kingdom, the title was often the crown prince and the title announced that the holder was the second ruler in the country. It is therefore sometimes translated as Hereditary or Crown Prince.

#2 Hereditary Princess (Iryt-pat)

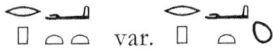

[hieroglyphs] var. [hieroglyphs]

r-pat, iryt-pat 'Princess, Noble, Heir (feminine)'

#3 King's Great Wife (Nesw Hemet Weret)

[hieroglyphs]

nsw Hmt wrt 'King's Great Wife'

King's Great Wife is the term that was used to refer to the principal wife of the pharaoh of Ancient Egypt. While most Ancient Egyptians were monogamous, the pharaoh would have had other, lesser wives and concubines in addition to the Great Royal Wife. This arrangement would allow the pharaoh to enter into diplomatic marriages with the daughters of allies, as was the custom of ancient kings.

The order of succession to the throne in Ancient Egypt passed through the royal women. The throne could also pass to the eldest living son of the pharaoh. The mother of the heir to the throne was not always the Great Royal Wife, but once a pharaoh was crowned, it was possible to grant the mother of the king the title of Great Royal Wife, along with other titles.

#4 God's Wife of Amun (Hemet Netjer en Amun)

Hmt nTr n Imn

'God's Wife of Amun'

The God's Wife of Amun was the highest-ranking priestess of the Amun cult at Thebes. The office had political religious importance, since the two were closely related in Ancient Egypt. Although the title first appears in the Middle Kingdom, its full political potential was not realized until the advent of Egypt's 18th dynasty. The title of God's Wife of Amun first appeared during the Tenth and Twelfth dynasties, when the title and position was held by non-royal women among those serving the gods Min, Amun, and Ptah as priestesses. At the beginning of the New Kingdom the title started to be held by royal women, usually by the wife of the king, but sometimes by the mother of the king, during this time its extreme power and prestige became evident.

The title, God's Wife of Amun, 'referred to the myth of the divine birth of the king, according to which his mother was impregnated by the god Amun.' The title holder was usually the King's Great Wife through whom the royal lineage ran. Ceremoniously and in reality the King who represented the carnate god Amun, impregnated his royal wife, the God's Wife of Amun, thus procuring the next god-pharaoh and heir to the throne, the Prince Elect, the Heir Apparent.

The first royal wife to hold this new title was Queen Ahmose-Nefertari, the wife of Ahmose I, this event is recorded in a stela in the temple of Amun at Karnak. She then passed it on to her daughter Merytamun, who in turn handed it to Hatshepsut, who used it before she ascended the throne as pharaoh.

Women who held the title of God's Wife of Amun during the end of the 17th Dynasty and the New Kingdom 18th Dynasty Period:

Ahhotep I: wife of Seqenenra Tao II and mother of Ahmose, the title God's Wife only appears on her coffin, first to hold this title.

Ahmose Nefertari: daughter of Seqenenra Tao II and sister-wife of Ahmose, first royal woman known to hold the office.

Satkamose: probably a daughter of Kamose, may have become God's Wife only posthumously.

Ahmose-Merytamun: daughter of Ahmose and sister-wife of Amenhotep I.

Ahmose Satamun: daughter of Ahmose, represented as a colossal statue in front of the eight pylon at Karnak.

Hatshepsut: daughter of Tuthmosis I and Queen Ahmose, given title of Divine Adoratrice of Amun also, became pharaoh.

Neferura: daughter of Tuthmosis II and Queen-Pharaoh Hatshepsut, possibly first royal wife of Tuthmosis III.

Iset: mother of Tuthmosis III, received the title of God's Wife after her death.

Satiah: next wife of Tuthmosis III in the early part of his reign.

Merytra-Hatshepsut: next wife of Tuthmosis III, mother of his heir, she was the daughter of the Divine Adoratrice of Amun Huy.

Merytamun: daughter of Tuthmosis III and Merytra-Hatshepsut.

Tiaa: wife of Amenhotep II and mother of Tuthmosis IV.

#5 God's Wife (Hemet Netjer)

𓊹𓏏𓈎

Hmt nTr

'God's Wife'

The shorter version of the title God's Wife was in use by the time of the Twelfth Dynasty, when the title is attested for the non-royal women Iy-meret-nebes and Neferu. As early as the First Intermediate Period there is mention of a 'Wife of the God' in reference to the god Min. The full title of 'God's Wife of Amun' is only used during and after the Eighteenth dynasty.

The title God's Wife was often allocated to royal women during the 18th Dynasty of Egypt. The term indicates an inherited sacral role, in which the role of 'God's Wife' passed from mother to daughter. The role could also exist among siblings, as in the case of the role of 'God's Wife' being shared or passed by daughters of Ahmose-Nefertari, Satamun (I) and her sister, Ahmose-Merytamun.

Despite certain allegations found online, the role of 'God's Wife' is not the same as the title 'God's Wife of Amun,' which is a separate sacral title, involved in the 'Divine Cycle' myth of the god Amun. Only two 18th Dynasty queens held this title, being Ahhotep and Ahmose-Nefertari

#6 Divine Adoratrice (Duat Netjer)

𓂧𓊹𓏏

dwAt nTr

'Divine Adorer, Praiser of the God'

The Divine Adoratrice of Amun was a second title created for the chief priestess of the ancient Egyptian deity, Amun. During the first millennium BC, when the holder of this office exercised her largest measure of influence, her position was an important appointment facilitating the transfer of power from one pharaoh to the next. The Divine Adoratrice ruled over the extensive temple duties and domains, controlling a significant part of the ancient Egyptian economy.

#7 King's Ornament-Concubine (Khekeret Nesut)

𓇓𓊪

nswt Xkrt

king insignia-ornament-concubine

'The King's Ornament-Concubine'

The King's Ornament (Concubine) is a much debated Ancient Egyptian woman's title. Women with this title are known from the First Intermediate Period, less often from the Middle Kingdom, but again often from the Second Intermediate Period and the New Kingdom. The title is often translated as 'Lady in Waiting' or 'King's Ornament.'

The title holders are most often married women of high status. In the Eleventh Dynasty, some queens of Mentjuhotep II had that title. These women may have been part of the king's harem, his concubines.

The name Khekeret, translates as:

Xkrt 'Coiffeuse (female hairdresser), concubine'

#8 United with the White Crown (Khenemet-neferet-Hedjet)

Xnmt-nfr-Hmt

united-good-white crown

'United with the White Crown'

Khenemet-Nefer-Hedjet was an ancient Egyptian queenly title during the Middle Kingdom. It was in use from the 12th to the early 18th dynasty. During the 12th dynasty it also occurred as a personal name. Its meaning is 'united with the white crown.' The white crown was one part of the double crown of Egypt and is usually interpreted to have represented Upper Egypt in the south.

#9 The Vizier - Prime Minister (Tjaty)

abbreviated: TAty 'Vizier'

The Vizier (Tjaty) was the highest official in Ancient Egypt to serve the king, or pharaoh during the Old, Middle, and New Kingdoms. The Instruction of Rekhmira (Installation of the Vizier), a New Kingdom text, defines many of the duties of the Tjaty, and lays down codes of behaviour. The viziers were often appointed by the pharaoh, most from loyalty or talent.

The vizier's most important duty was to supervise the running of the country, such as a prime minister, at times even small details of it such as sampling the city's water supply. All other lesser supervisors and officials, such as tax collectors and scribes, would report to the vizier. The judiciary was part of the civil administration and the vizier also sat in the High Court. However at any time, the pharaoh could exert his own control over any aspect of government, overriding the vizier's decisions. The vizier also supervised the security of the pharaoh and the palace. They often acted as the pharaoh's seal bearer as well, and the vizier would record trade. In the New Kingdom, there were two viziers, one for Upper Egypt and one for Lower Egypt.

#10 Viceroy of Kush (Sa Neswt en Kash)

nsw sA n kAS

King son of Kash

'King's Son of Kash (Kush, Nubian Kingdom)'

#11 Scribe (Sesh)

𓋴𓏏𓏝

sS

'Scribe'

Scribes were not always priests, but it might be said that most priests were scribes and that many functions in the temples required the skills of a scribe.

The middle hieroglyph in the name is the scribes writing apparatus of reed, water pot and palette.

Scribes were educated in the 'House of Life' (Per Ankh) where they also carried out a great deal of their profession. Mostly they used the hieratic (cursive form of the hieroglyphic) which was a faster form of writing as opposed to the more formal hieroglyphs. In the 'House of Life' scribes studied and copied the sacred texts which were kept there. We do not know for sure, but it seems likely that some teaching was given there too. There is a record of one 'Teacher of the House of Life' at Abydos. Scribes would have kept ancient texts necessary for the cult, copying and correcting older documents. They also prepared theological and liturgical texts particular to the temple they worked at. Apart from this, they prepared books of magical spells and astronomical tables and prepared huge numbers of the 'Book of Going Forth by Day.'

𓇓𓋴𓏏𓏝 nsw sS 'King's Scribe'

#12 Lector Priest (Khery-Hebet)

⌒𓂋𓏤𓏏𓊖𓏛 var. 𓏛𓂋𓏛

Xry-Hbt

'Lector Priest, literally: Holder of the Ritual Book'

A lector priest, in ancient Egypt, was a priest who recited spells and hymns during official ceremonies, such as temple rituals. Such priests also sold their services to laymen, reciting texts during private magical rituals to ward off evil or bad luck or at funerals. They were some of the most prominent practitioners of 'magic' (𓎛𓎡𓄿𓏛 HkA) in ancient Egypt. In ancient Egyptian literature, lector priests are often portrayed as the keepers of secret knowledge and the performers of amazing magical feats.

The highest-ranking lector priest in a temple, the chief lector priest, managed the temple's archives of ritual texts.

The term 'lector priest' literally means 'the carrier of the book of rituals.' The term for a chief lector priest, Xry-Hbt, Hry-tp, was so closely associated with magic that, in Late Egyptian, the shortened form Hry-tp became a general term for 'magician.' Lector priests wore a sash across the chest that indicated their position.

#13 Local Prince-Mayor (Haty-a)

𓄂𓏤𓏏𓇌𓀀

HAty-a

'Count, regional governor, mayor, Nomarch of a regional Nome'

Literally 'man at the front, at the head'

Ḥaty-a was an ancient Egyptian rank and title given to local princes, mayors, or governors.

#14 Local Princess-Female Nomarch (Hatet-a)

HAtt-a

'Female Nomarch, Chieftess of a regional Nome'

Literally 'woman at the front, at the head'

#15 Chief-Nomarch (Hery-tep)

'Chief, nomarch'

#16 Great Chief - Nomarch (Hery-tep-aa)

Hry-tp-aA

'Nomarch, literally: Great Head chief'

Nomarchs were the rulers of Ancient Egyptian provinces (Nomes) Serving as provincial governors, they each held authority over one of the 42 Nomes into which the country was divided:

Sepat: ⟨hieroglyphs⟩ spAt 'Nome, province, district'

#17 Fan Bearer (Tjaw-khu)

⟨hieroglyphs⟩

tAw-xw

'Fan Bearer'

This was an important position in the royal court, one who was close to the king.

#18 Fan Bearer On the Hand of the King

(Tjaw-khu Her-wenemy-a en Nesw)

⟨hieroglyphs⟩

TAw-xw, Hr-wnmy-a n nsw

fan-bearer, upon right-hand king

'Fan Bearer Upon the Right Hand of the King'

The Viceroy of Kush Amenhotep called Huy holding the long fan with the single feather indicating his rank as fan-bearer

The Fan-bearer on the Right Hand of the King was an Ancient Egyptian courtier.

The title denotes a very close personal or official relationship with the king. During the times of Amenhotep II and Tuthmosis IV the title was held by officials like the viceroy of Kush, the chief steward of the king, and several tutors, such as Sennedjem under Tutankhamun. Scenes depicting the fan-bearers show them holding a long fan with a single feather.

#19 Priest - Servant of the God (Hem-Netjer)

𓍹𓏏 Hm-nTr servant-god 'Servant of the God, Priest'

This is the oldest clerical title, known from the 1st Dynasty. These priests prepared and carried forward offerings to the god and assisted at ceremonies and processions. They had access to the sanctuary where the divine image was kept, and controlled the entrance to the temple. Some of the large cult centres with a great number of Servants of God had overseers or high priests of the priesthood.

#20 High Priest of Osiris (Hem-Netjer-en-Wesir)

𓍹𓏏𓏤𓊨

Hm-nTr-n-wsir

Servant-god-of-Osiris

'High Priest of Osiris'

The High Priest of Osiris served as head of the cult of Osiris at Abydos. In ancient Egypt, a high priest was the chief priest of any of the many gods revered by the Egyptians.

#21 High Priests of Amun (Hem-Netjer en Amun)

𓊹𓏤𓈖𓏤𓇳

Hm-nTr   n imn

Servant-god of Amun

'High Priest of Amun (Ra), literally 'Servant of the god Amun (Ra)'

The main cult of Amun was in Thebes.

Theban High Priests of Amun, while not regarded as a dynasty, the High Priests of Amun at Thebes were nevertheless of such power and influence that they were effectively the rulers of Upper Egypt from 1080 to 943 BC.

The High Priest of Amun or First Prophet of Amun (hem netjer en tepy) was the highest-ranking priest in the priesthood of the Ancient Egyptian god Amun. The first high priests of Amun appear in the New Kingdom, at the beginning of the Eighteenth Dynasty.

The priesthood of Amun rose in power during the early Eighteenth dynasty through significant tributes to the god Amun by rulers such as Hatshepsut and more importantly Thutmose III. The Amun priesthood in Thebes had four high-ranking priests:

The high priest of Amun at Karnak (hm netjer tepy en Amun): also referred to as the first prophet of Amun.

The second priest of Amun at Karnak (hm netjer sen-nu en Amun): also referred to as the second prophet of Amun.

The third priest of Amun at Karnak (hm netjer khemet-nu en Amun): also referred to as the third prophet of Amun.

231

The fourth priest of Amun at Karnak (hm netjer fed-nu en Amun): also referred to as the fourth prophet of Amun.

#22 High Priest of Ptah:

𓄿𓏭𓏤

wr-xrp-Hmww

great-controller-craftsmen

'High Priest of Ptah, literally: Great Controller of the Craftsmen'

The main cult of Ptah was in Memphis. The High Priest of Ptah was sometimes referred to as the Greatest of the Masters of the Craftsmen. This title refers to Ptah as the patron god of the craftsmen. The office of the High Priest of Ptah was located in Memphis. The temple of Ptah in Memphis was dedicated to Ptah, his consort Sekhmet and their son Nefertem.

#23 Sem Priest of Ptah (Sem)

𓂟𓄿

sm

'Sem Priest (of Ptah)'

It was common for the high priest to also hold the title of sem-priest of Ptah. The sem-priest could be recognized by the fact that he wore a short wig with a side-lock and was dressed in a panther skin. The Sem Priest performed the 'Opening of the Mouth' ceremony at the diseased pharaoh's mummy during the ritual burial. This was performed using a sacred adze which 'splits open' the deceased's mouth to enable speech in the afterlife. This office and ceremony was usually performed by the eldest son, the Heir Apparent.

The Opening of the Mouth Ritual performed on Tutankhamun's mummy. The new pharaoh Ay, dressed as a Sem-Priest, performing the Opening of the Mouth ceremony on the Mummy of Tutankhamun. At the end of his long funeral, there was one last rite to be performed before the young king's mummified body could be finally laid in its coffin and sealed up in his burial chamber. It was called the 'Opening of the Mouth.' The Egyptians believed this ceremony was absolutely essential to reanimate a person's ka (life force), so that in the afterlife the dead could once again be in full possession of their senses, and thereby once again be able to taste and to speak, breathe and smell, see, hear, and touch. The ceremony involved an elaborate ritual that scholars believe involved at least 75 separate steps, such as touching the mummy's mouth nose, eyes, and ears with a variety of tools and instruments, including an adze, a chisel, a peshkef (a flint knife shaped like a fishtail) and a netjeri knife made from meteoric iron.

This painting from the wall of Pharaoh Tutankhamun's Tomb may have been a brilliant piece of political propaganda. For by showing himself performing on the dead king the ceremony of the Opening of the Mouth, Ay helped to prove his claim to the throne of Egypt. Because a dead man's oldest son and heir traditionally took on this role dressed in the leopard-skin costume of a sem-priest, this painting declares that Ay was Tutankhamun's legitimate successor as pharaoh, a claim stated also by Ay's khepresh (Blue War) crown. Every detail testifies to his claim, despite the fact that Ay was not of royal blood, and though a high-ranking official who served the king as his vizier, he was only a commoner and not a blood relative of the king. Ay may even have seized the throne from Horemheb, the man everyone assumed would be Tutankhamun's heir and successor as pharaoh. He soon would be, in fact, when just four years later Ay himself lay dead.

#24 High Priest of Ra (Wer-Hemu)

wr-Hmw

great-seer

'Greatest of Seers (High Priest of Ra)'

The High Priest of Ra was known in Egyptian as the **wr-Hmw**, which translates as 'Greatest of Seers.'

The main cult of Ra was in ancient Heliopolis, northeast of present day Cairo. The high priests of Ra are not as well documented as the high priests of other deities such as Amun and Ptah.

#25 Chief Steward - Great Overseer of the House (Imy-r-per-wer)

imy-r pr wr

overseer house great

'Great Overseer of the house, Chief Steward'

The Chief Steward or Great Overseer of the House was an important official at the royal court in Ancient Egypt in the Middle Kingdom and in the New Kingdom.   He was the main person in charge of the estates supplying the palace and the royal residence with food.

#26 Servant in the Place of Truth (Sedjem-ash em Set Maat)

sDm-aS m st mAat

Servant in place truth

'Servant in the Place of Truth'

Sedjem-ash em set maat is translated as 'Servant in the Place of Truth' is an Ancient Egyptian title that is used to refer to someone who worked in the Theban Necropolis, on the west bank of the Nile in Thebes.

The word sDm-aS contains the words:

sDm: 'to hear, to obey'

aS: 'to summon, to call out'

235

So the phrase **sDm-aS** literally means 'one who listens to the command and obeys,' hence it is translated as 'servant.'

#27 Treasurer - Chancellor - Overseer of the Seal (Imy-r Khetemet)

imy-r xtmt

overseer seal

'Treasurer, literally: Overseer of the Seal, or Overseer of Sealed Things'

The office of 'Overseer of the Seal' is known since the end of the Old Kingdom, where people with this title appear sporadically in the organization of private estates. In the Middle Kingdom the office became one of the most important ones at the royal court. At the end of the 18th Dynasty the title lost its importance. In the later New Kingdom the function of a treasurer was overtaken by the overseer of the treasury. The treasurer was responsible for products coming to the royal palace. They were the main economic administrators of the royal belongings.

There words for seal are:

 sDAwt 'seal'

 sDAyt 'seal'

xtm 'seal'

The word **Sedjaut** or **Khetemet** 'Treasurer, Seal Bearer' can be abbreviated as:

☒ or ⌂

Ptahmose was the High Priest of Ptah in Memphis during the reign of Thutmose III who held the title of 'Great Seal Bearer of the King of Lower Egypt':

𓈖𓎛𓅭𓄜 bity xtmt wr 'Great Seal Bearer of the King of the North.'

He was accredited with other titles which included 'Hereditary Prince, Count and Sem-Priest.'

b. 70038.

Naos with statue of the High Priest of Ptah Ptahmose, who served under Thutmose III. Black granite (H. cm 80), from Abydos, reign of Thutmose III, 18th dynasty, New Kingdom. Cairo, Egyptian Museum.

237

The inscription on the hem of his kilt reads:

bity xtmt wrt, sxm imnt, ptH-ms

King-North Treasurer Great, Controller West, Ptah-mose

'Great Seal Bearer of the King of the North, Ptah-mose'

#28 The Scarab of Princess Gilukhepa:

HAt-sep 10 xr Hm n Hr

'Regnal Year 10 under the Majesty of the Horus...'

This is followed by the full titles of Amenhotep III:

'Strong Bull appearing in Truth, He of the Two Goddesses, Establishing Laws, Pacifying the Two Lands, Golden Horus, Great of Valour, Smiting the Asiatics, King of Upper and Lower Egypt, Neb-Maat-Ra, Son of Ra, Amenhotep, Ruler of Thebes, given Life, the King's Great Wife:'

nsw Hmt wrt (Ty) anx ti

'King's Great Wife (Ty) may she Live.'

rn n it.s YwiA, rn n mwt.s TwiA

'The name of her father, Yuia, the name of her mother, Tjuia.'

tm ywt ini n n ywt n Hm.f anx-wDA-snb

'Marvel brought to his Majesty, Life, Prosperity and Health.'

sAt smsw n NhrnA, Sa-ti-r-nA

'The daughter-elder, of the Prince of Naharina, Shutarna'

Kyr-gy-pA tp-st(w) n xnr.s, st 317

'Gilukhepa, chief women of her harem,

three hundred and seventeen women.'

239

http://arkpublising.co.uk

Printed in Great Britain
by Amazon